The Gardener's Palette

The Gardener's Palette

A Year of Color in the Flower Garden

Pierre Nessmann
Brigitte & Philippe Perdereau

Stewart, Tabori & Chang
New York

Published in 2008 by Stewart, Tabori & Chang
An imprint of Harry N. Abrams, Inc.

Library of Congress Cataloging-in-Publication Data

Nessmann, Pierre.
  The gardener's palette : a year of color in the flower garden / by Pierre Nessmann ;
  photographs by Brigitte and Philippe Perdereau.
    p. cm.
  Includes bibliographical references and index.
  ISBN 13: 978-1-58479-644-2
  ISBN 10: 1-58479-644-8
  1. Color in gardening. 2. Flower gardening. 3. Flowers—Color. I. Perdereau, Brigitte.
  II. Perdereau, Philippe. III. Title.

SB454.3.C64N47 2008
635.9'68—dc22

                          2007033163

Translated by Krister Swartz

Project Manager, English-language edition: Magali Veillon
Editor, English-language edition: Miranda Ottewell
Designer, English-language edition: Shawn Dahl
Production Manager, English-language edition: Tina Cameron

The text of this book was composed in Profile.

Printed and bound in France by Pollina - L 45244
10 9 8 7 6 5 4 3 2 1

HNA
harry n. abrams, inc.
a subsidiary of La Martinière Groupe

115 West 18th Street
New York, NY 10011
www.hnabooks.com

CONTENTS

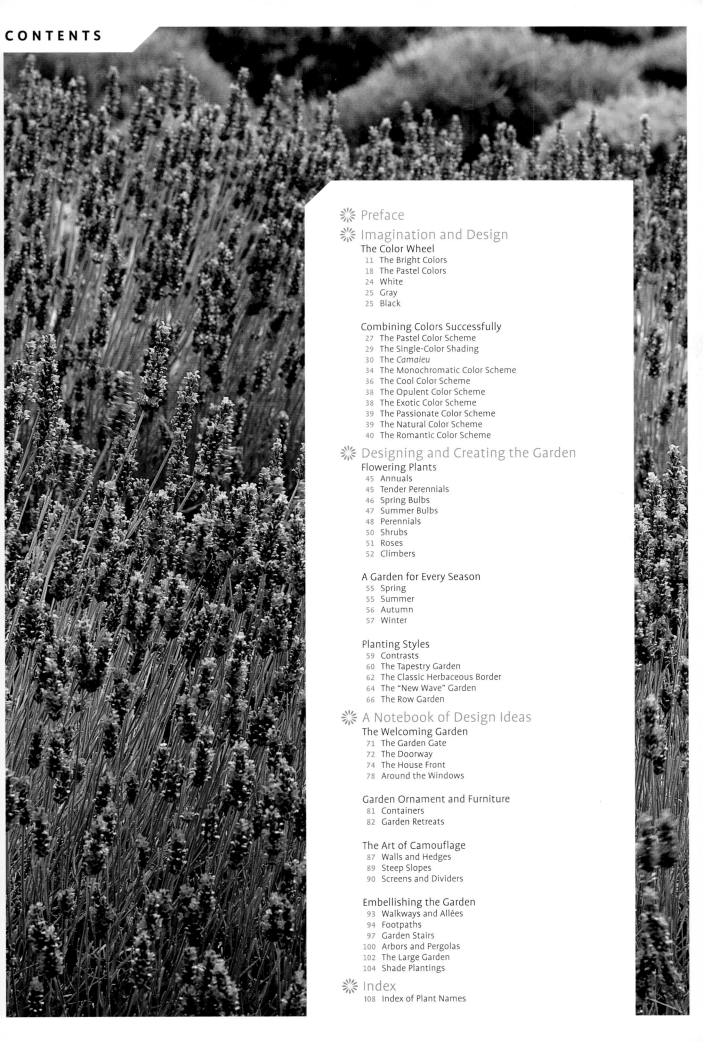

Like a painter, the gardener has a large range of
colors at his disposal to create his compositions.
Where the painter uses tubes of paint, the gardener
uses the living color of flowers and foliage. But the
gardener must know more than just how to choose
colors; he also needs to know how to combine them
in a harmonious way. Art is based on a few aesthetic
principles that govern the choice of colors and their
combinations, but it also relies on the sensibilities
of each artist. Similarly, the emotions that one feels
while looking at a flower bed, far from being acci-
dental, are the result of patient work assembling
the colors of flowers and foliage into a harmonious
whole, a long-drawn-out process by which the
gardener hopes to approach perfection. A few cele-
brated landscape artists, such as Gertrude Jekyll, a
pioneer in the art of color combinations and flower
border design, have defined the basic rules that still
guide us today. With true gardening, we are not
satisfied with merely filling in the space of a flower
border, but instead try to employ the infinite variety
of flowering plants with their enchanting range of
hues to give each bed a a sense of meaning. ■

Imagination and Design

✳ Color is a sensation caused by the action of light on the retina. In theory, when a ray of white light traverses a glass prism, it reveals an array of seven colors. In real life, this can be seen at the end of a rainstorm, when a multitude of small droplets of water collected in the atmosphere refract light to form a rainbow. From violet blue to magenta red, and passing through cyan blue, green, yellow, orange, and orange red, the colors found in this rainbow form the color spectrum. To better understand their relationship to each other, these colors can be assembled in a color wheel, in which the colors are further divided. From the base of the three primary colors—magenta red, cyan blue, and yellow—a great number of shades grouped into secondary and tertiary colors can be found in the color wheel. Add the neutral tones of white, gray, and black to this palette of twelve colors, and you come up with an infinite variety of colors. This richness of hue present in the world of the arts is also found in the world of plants, where flowers can be found in a limitless multitude of shades. ■

The Color Wheel

☀ **A palette of flowers to express the language of colors.** The color wheel gathers together colors thought of as hot, from yellow through orange and on to scarlet red, and those referred to as cold, from green to purplish red, with an array of different shades of blue and mauve in between. Pastel colors are created by softening bright colors with varying proportions of white to make up a range of more or less pale colors. The color charts on the following pages provide a list of flowers that correspond to a range of color samples. ∎

The Bright Colors

Lemon Yellow

Annuals
African marigold, *Tagetes erecta* 'Antigua Prime Rose,' 'Doubloon'
French marigold, *Tagetes patula* 'Lemon Yellow'
Sunflower, *Helianthus annuus* 'Lemon Queen'

Bulbs
Daffodil, *Narcissus*
Dahlia 'Boy Mick,' 'Mark Harwick' (above), 'Yellow Spider'
Tulip, *Tulipa*

Perennials
Basket-of-gold, *Alyssum saxatile*
Bearded iris, *Iris germanica* 'Findekind'
Daylily, *Hemerocallis* 'Corky'
Elecampane, *Inula helenium*
Garden loosestrife, *Lysimachia punctata*
Ox-eye daisy, *Buphthalmum salicifolium*
Pheasant's eye, *Adonis vernalis*
Siberian spurge, *Euphorbia seguieriana* ssp. *niciciana*
Tree lupine, *Lupinus arboreus*

Shrubs
Pineapple broom, *Cytisus battandieri*
Provence broom, *Genista purgans*
Shower tree, *Cassia corymbosa*
Spanish broom, *Genista hispanica*
St.-John's-wort, *Hypericum patulum* 'Hidcote'
Swamp azalea, *Rhododendron viscosum* 'Arpège'

Climbers
Honeysuckle, *Lonicera x brownii* 'Golden Trumpet'

Golden Yellow

Annuals
Coneflower, *Rudbeckia* 'Maya'
French marigold, *Tagetes patula* 'Golden Jubilee'
Million bells, *Calibrachoa* 'Callie'
Nasturtium, *Tropaeolum* 'Vesuvius'
Signet marigold, *Tagetes tenuifolia* 'Gnome'
Sunflower, *Helianthus annuus* 'Angel's Halo'

Bulbs
Canna 'Louis Cottin'
Daffodil, *Narcissus* 'Fortune'
Dahlia 'Garden Party,' 'Border Princess'

Perennials
Avens, *Geum chiloense* 'Lady Stratheden'
Coneflower, *Rudbeckia fulgida* 'Goldsturm'
Cushion spurge, *Euphorbia polychroma*
Daylily, *Hemerocallis* 'By Myself'
Gazania pinnata
Globeflower, *Trollius chinensis* 'Golden Queen'
Goldenrod, *Solidago* 'Mimosa'
Inula hookerii
Ligularia dentata 'Desdemona'
Red hot poker, *Kniphofia* 'Butter Cup'
Sedum kamtschaticum
Tickseed, *Coreopsis grandiflora* 'Early Sunrise'

Shrubs
Azalea, *Rhododendron mollis* 'Lingot d'Or'
Cinquefoil, *Potentilla* 'Tangerine'
Rose, *Rosa* 'Gene Tierney' (above)
Warminster broom, *Cytisus x praecox* 'Allgold'

Orange

Annuals
African daisy, *Arctotis* 'Harlequin'
French marigold, *Tagetes patula* 'Orange'
Pot marigold, *Calendula* 'Little Ball Orange'
Signet marigold, *Tagetes tenuifolia* 'Tangerine Gem'
Sunflower, *Helianthus annuus* 'Soraya'

Bulbs
Canna 'Wyoming'
Dahlia 'Hamari Gold,' 'Melody Swing'
Tuberous begonia, *Begonia x tuberhybrida* 'Panorama Orange'
Tulip, *Tulipa* 'General de Wet' (above)

Perennials
Avens, *Geum chiloense* 'Princess Juliana'
Daylily, *Hemerocallis fulva* 'Flore Pleno,' *H.* 'Burning Daylight'
Globeflower, *Trollius* 'Princess Orange'
Monkey flower, *Mimulus glutinosus*
Peruvian lily, *Alstroemeria aurea* 'Orange King'
Red hot poker, *Kniphofia* 'Little Elf'
St. John's chamomile, *Anthemis sancti-johannis*
Sunflower, *Helianthemum* 'Fire Dragon'
Welsh poppy, *Meconopsis cambrica* var. *aurantiaca*

Shrubs
Barberry, *Berberis darwinii*
Butterfly bush, *Buddleia x weyeriana* 'Sungold'
Cinquefoil, *Potentilla fruticosa* 'Red Ace'
Rose, *Rosa* 'Souvenir de J. B. Guillot'

Climbers
Trumpet creeper, *Campsis grandiflora*

Orange-Red

Annuals and Biennials
Bedding geranium, *Pelargonium zonale* 'Signal'
Cosmos sulphureus 'Sunny Red'
Impatiens 'Cahuita'
Mexican sunflower, *Tithonia speciosa* 'Torch'
Pansy, *Viola* 'Angel Sweet Pea,' 'Chantreyland'
Zinnia 'Golden State'

Bulbs
Dahlia 'Akita,' 'Trelawny'
Tulip, *Tulipa* 'Compostella'

Perennials
Avens, *Geum chiloense* 'Fire Opal'
Butterfly weed, *Asclepias tuberosa*
Campion, *Lychnis x arkwrightii* 'Vesuvius'
Chrysanthemum 'Orange Wonder'
Cinquefoil, *Potentilla* 'W. Rollisson'
Croscosmia 'Babylon,' 'James Coey'
Garden phlox, *Phlox paniculata*
   'Orange Perfection'
Griffith's spurge, *Euphorbia griffithii* 'Fire Glow'
Lion's ear, *Leonotis leonurus*
Lotus 'Fire Vine'
Orange fleabane, *Erigeron aurantiacus*
Yarrow, *Achillea millefolium* 'Paprika' (above)

Shrubs
Flowering quince, *Chaenomeles speciosa*
   'Friesdorfer'
Scotch broom, *Cytisus scoparius* 'Paulette'
Rose, *Rosa* 'Spice Twice'

Climbers
Trumpet creeper, *Campsis x tagliabuana*
   'Mme Galen'

Coral Red

Annuals
Impatiens 'Coral'
Nasturtium, *Tropaeolum* 'Scarlet Gleam'
Scarlet sage, *Salvia splendens* 'Bloody Mary,'
   'Fire Star'

Bulbs
Dahlia 'Kenora Valentine,' 'Red Pigmy'
Gladiolus 'Traderhorn'
Tuberous begonia, *Begonia bertinii*
Tulip, *Tulipa* 'Apeldoorn,' 'Red Riding Hood'

Perennials
Astilbe arendsii 'Etna'
Beard tongue, *Penstemon* 'Southgate Gem'
Cape fuchsia, *Phygelius capensis*
Coral bells, *Heuchera x brizoides* 'Pluie de Feu'
Garden phlox, *Phlox paniculata* 'Starfire'
Lobelia fulgens 'Elmfeuer'
Mullein, *Verbascum* 'Cherry Helen'
Oriental poppy, *Papaver orientale* 'Allegro'
Red hot poker, *Kniphofia* 'Alcazar' (above)

Shrubs
Kurume azalea, *Rhododendron kurume*
   'Hino Crimson'
Pomegranate, *Punica granatum*
Yellow sage, *Lantana camara*

Climbers
Clematis 'Vino'
Trumpet creeper, *Campsis radicans*

Red

Annuals
Bedding geranium, *Pelargonium* 'Moulin Rouge'
French marigold, *Tagetes patula* 'Durango Red'
Scarlet sage, *Salvia splendens* 'Cover Girl'
Zinnia tenuifolia 'Red Spider'

Bulbs
Canna 'Tafraout'
Dahlia 'Stephan Bergerdorff'
Tuberous begonia, *Begonia multiflora*
   'Switzerland'
Tulip, *Tulipa* 'Ile-de-France'

Perennials
Astilbe arendsii 'Spinell'
Avens, *Geum chiloense* 'Mrs. Bradshaw'
Bee balm, *Monarda* 'Cambridge Scarlet'
Cardinal flower, *Lobelius cardinalis*
   'Queen Victoria'
Crocosmia 'Lucifer'
Daylily, *Hemerocallis* 'Allan'
Lupine, *Lupinus* 'Mon Château'
Maltese cross, *Lychnis chalcedonica*
Mountain fleece, *Persicaria amplexicaulis*
   'Atropurpureum'
Oriental poppy, *Papaver orientale* 'Goliath' (above)
Peony, *Paeonia* 'Felix Crousse'
Peruvian verbena, *Verbena peruvianum*
Prairie mallow, *Sidalcea malviflora* 'Interlaken'
Rock cress, *Aubrieta* 'Bressingham Red'
Rose campion, *Lychnis coronaria*
Rose mallow, *Hibiscus moscheutos*

Shrubs
Baby sage, *Salvia microphylla*
Mophead hydrangea, *Hydrangea macrophylla*
   'Red Cap'
Weigelia 'Red Prince'

Deep Red

Annuals
Cosmos 'Dazzler'
Cuphea 'Tiny Mice'
Nasturtium, *Tropaeolum* 'Empress of India'
Petunia 'Storm Red'

Bulbs
Canna 'Black Night'
Dahlia 'Gallery Singer'

Perennials
Astilbe arendsii 'Etna'
Beard tongue, *Penstemon* 'Port Wine'
Cinquefoil, *Potentilla astrosanguinea*
Cottage pink, *Dianthus plumarius* 'Desmond'
New York aster, *Aster novi-belgii* 'Royal Ruby'
Oriental poppy, *Papaver orientale* 'Beauty of
    Livermore'
Pasque flower, *Pulsatilla vulgaris* 'Rubra'
Red valerian, *Centranthus ruber* 'Coccineus'
Sun rose, *Helianthemum* 'Fire Ball'

Shrubs
Azalea, *Rhododendron* 'Mothers' Day'
Camellia japonica 'Bella Lambertii'
Currant, *Ribes sanguineum* 'Koja'
Flowering quince, *Chaenomeles speciosa* 'Rubra'
Lilac, *Syringa vulgaris* 'Prince Wokonsky'
Rhododendron 'Nova Zembla'
Weeping bottlebrush, *Callistemon viminalis*
    'Little John'

Climbers
Clematis 'Jackmanii Rubra'
Morning glory, *Ipomoea purpurea* 'Scarlett O'Hara'
Sweet pea, *Lathyrus* 'Mandie Best' (above)

Burgundy

Annuals and Biennials
Chocolate cosmos, *Cosmos atrosanguinea*
Painted tongue, *Salpiglossis* 'Chocolate'
Pansy, *Viola* 'Barn Purple'
Rainbow pink, *Dianthus chinensis* 'Crimson'
Sweet William, *Dianthus barbatus* 'Noverna Violet'

Bulbs
Buttercup, *Ranunculus* 'Pauline Violet'
Dahlia 'El Nino'
Dragon arum, *Dracunculus vulgaris*
Drumstick allium, *Allium sphaerocephalum*
    (above)
Gladiolus 'Mexico'

Perennials
Bearded iris, *Iris germanica* 'Royal Knight,'
    'Cherry Garden'
Dark columbine, *Aquilegia atrata*
Daylily, *Hemerocallis* 'Chicago Royal Robe'
Knautia macedonica
Lenten rose, *Helleborus orientalis* 'Atrorubens'

Shrubs
Butterfly bush, *Buddleia davidii* 'Nanho Purple'
Lilac, *Syringa vulgaris* 'Charles Joly'
Rhododendron 'America'
Rose, *Rosa* 'Papa Meilland'

Climbers
Clematis 'Warsaw Nike'
Morning glory, *Ipomoea purpurea* 'Kniola's
    Black Knight'

Deepest Violet

Annuals
Petunia 'Pirouette Purple'
Scarlet sage, *Salvia splendens* 'Phoenix Purple'

Bulbs
Dahlia 'Rip City,' 'Arabian Night'

Perennials
Bearded iris, *Iris germanica* 'High Life'
Dark columbine, *Aquilegia atrata*
Daylily, *Hemerocallis* 'American Revolution'
Giant wild parsnip, *Angelica gigas* (above)
Mourning widow, *Geranium phaeum*
Pincushion flower, *Scabiosa caucasica*
    'Chile Black'

Shrubs
Lilac, *Syringa vulgaris* 'Souvenir de Louis Spaeth'
Spanish lavender, *Lavandula stoechas* ssp.
    Pedunculata

Climbers
Clematis 'Romantika'

Fuchsia

Annuals
Bedding geranium, *Pelargonium zonale* 'Bright Rose'
Cosmos 'Louvre'
Four-o'clock, *Mirabilis jalapa* 'Rose'
Lobelia maritima 'Deep Rose'

Bulbs
Dahlia 'Boy Scout,' 'Gallery Art Nouveau'
Gladiolus 'Violet Moon'

Perennials
Astilbe arendsii 'Cattleya'
Bergenia 'Abendglut'
Blazing star, *Liatris spicata* 'Floristan Violet'
Cottage pink, *Dianthus plumarius* 'Annabel,' 'Warden Hybrid'
Garden phlox, *Phlox paniculata* 'Tenor' (above)
Italian aster, *Aster amellus* 'Lady Hindip'
New England aster, *Aster novae-angliae* 'Rosanna'
Rock cress, *Arabis blepharophylla*
Shooting star, *Dodecatheon meadia*

Shrubs
Dwarf Russian almond, *Prunus tenella* 'Firehill'
Rhododendron 'Red Eye'
Spiraea x billardii

Climbers
Everlasting pea, *Lathyrus latifolius*

Deep Pink

Annuals
Petunia 'Cherry'
Scarlet sage, *Salvia splendens* 'Lavender Vista'
Zinnia 'Purple Prince'

Bulbs
Gladiolus 'Violet Moon'

Perennials
Hardy geranium, *Geranium x riversleaianum* 'Russell Prichard'
Japanese anemone, *Anemone japonica* 'Prinz Heinrich'
Loosestrife, *Lythrum virgatum* 'Rose Queen'
New England aster, *Aster novae-angliae* 'Paul Gerber'
Sun rose, *Helianthemum* 'Ben Hope'
Wallflower, *Erysimum linifolium* 'Bowles Mauve'

Shrubs
Azalea, *Rhododendron japonica* 'Silvester'
Mophead hydrangea, *Hydrangea macrophylla* 'Merveille'
Purple rock rose, *Cistus purpureus*
Rose of Sharon, *Hibiscus syriacus* 'Pink Giant' (above)

Violet

Annuals
Petunia 'Twilight Blue'
Verbena 'Violet Blue Lace'
Wishbone flower, *Torenia* 'Large Violet'

Bulbs
Ornamental allium, *Allium giganteum* (above)

Perennials
Bee balm, *Monarda* 'Blaustrumpf'
Bushy aster, *Aster dumosus* 'Fidelio'
Hardy geranium, *Geranium himalayense* 'Gravette'
New York aster, *Aster novi-belgii* 'Sarah Ballard'
Pincushion flower, *Scabiosa columbaria* 'Butterfly Blue'
Rock cress, *Aubrieta* 'Drayton'
Speedwell, *Veronica longiflora* 'Blauriensin'
Spiderwort, *Tradescantia x andersoniana* 'Blue Stone'
Violet, *Viola suavis* 'Marie Louise'
Woodland sage, *Salvia nemorosa* 'Ostfriesland'

Shrubs
Bush clover, *Lespedeza thunbergii*
Lilac, *Syringa chinensis*
Rhododendron 'Praecox'

Climbers
Clematis 'Lord Nevill,' *C. integrifolia* 'Durandii'
Paper flower, *Bougainvillea glabra*

Dark Violet

Annuals
Bush violet, *Browallia speciosa* 'Ocean Violet'
Edging lobelia, *Lobelia erinus* 'Blue'
Larkspur, *Consolida ajacis* 'Purple'
Petunia 'Surfinia Blue'
Scarlet sage, *Salvia splendens* 'Phoenix Purple'

Perennials
Delphinium 'King Arthur'
Fleabane, *Erigeron* 'Dunkelste Aller'
High mallow, *Malva sylvestris* ssp. *mauritiana*
   (above)
Italian aster, *Aster amellus* 'Blue King'
Japanese iris, *Iris ensata* 'Dark Lightning'
Lobelia x *gerardii* 'Verdrariensis'
Skullcap, *Scutellaria baicalensis*
Woodland sage, *Salvia nemorosa* 'May Night'

Shrubs
Butterfly bush, *Buddleia davidii* 'Black Night'
Lavender, *Lavandula angustifolia* 'Hidcote'
Lilac, *Syringa vulgaris* 'Arthur William Paul'

Climbers
Clematis 'Multi Blue'

Ultramarine Blue

Annuals and Biennials
Edging lobelia, *Lobelia erinus* 'Marine Blue'
Forget-me-not, *Myosotis alpestris* 'Miro'
Larkspur, *Consolida ajacis* 'Blue Spire'
Love-in-a-mist, *Nigella damascena* 'Blue Crown'
Mealycup sage, *Salvia farinacea* 'Midi'
Nemesia 'Blue'
Pansy, *Viola* 'Deep Blue,' 'Lambada Midnight Blue'

Perennials
Bugloss, *Anchusa azurea* 'Royal Blue'
Clustered bellflower, *Campanula glomerata*
   'Superba'
Globe thistle, *Echinops ritro* 'Blue Star'
Hardy geranium, *Geranium* 'Orion'
Heliotrope, *Heliotropium peruvianum* 'Incense'
Italian aster, *Aster amellus* 'Catherine'
Lily of the Nile, *Agapanthus* 'Bressingham Blue'
Speedwell, *Veronica austriaca* ssp. *teucrium* 'Crater
   Lake Blue'

Shrubs
California lilac, *Ceanothus impressus* 'Puget Blue'
Mophead hydrangea, *Hydrangea macrophylla*
   'Mathilde Gutges' (above)

Climbers
Clematis 'Daniel Deronda,' 'Hendersonii'

Violet-Blue

Annuals
Edging lobelia, *Lobelia erinus* 'Midnight Blue'
Fan flower, *Scaevola* 'Saphira'
Million bells, *Calibrachoa* 'Trailing Blue'
Petunia 'Royal Velvet'
Pimpernel, *Anagallis* 'Skylover'
Summer snapdragon, *Angelonia* 'Blue'

Bulbs
Crocus vernus 'Purpurea'
Hyacinth, *Hyacinthus* 'Blue Magic,' 'Delft Blue'

Perennials
Bearded iris, *Iris germanica* 'Royal Touch' (above)
Blue-eyed grass, *Sisyrinchium bermudianum*
Delphinium 'Blue Bird'
East Indies aster, *Aster tongolensis* 'Goliath'
Heliotrope, *Heliotropium peruvianum*
Rock cress, *Aubrieta* 'Dr. Mules'
Woodland sage, *Salvia nemorosa* 'Blue Queen'

Shrubs
Butterfly bush, *Buddleia davidii* 'Empire Blue,'
   'Nanho Blue'
Chaste tree, *Vitex agnus-castus*
English lavender, *Lavandula angustifolia*
   'Munstead'

Climbers
Morning glory, *Ipomoea purpurea* 'Grandpa Ott'

Indigo Blue

Annuals and Biennials
Edging lobelia, *Lobelia erinus* 'Sky Blue'
Forget-me-not, *Myosotis alpestris* 'Ultramarine,'
  'Wagner's Perfecta'
Pimpernel, *Anagallis grandiflora* 'Blue Light'

Bulbs
Grape hyacinth, *Muscari armeniacum*
Squill, *Scilla sibirica*

Perennials
Bellflower, *Campanula collina*
Dayflower, *Commelina tuberosa*
Delphinium 'Blue Bird,' 'Tom Pouce'
Gentian, *Gentiana acaulis*
Gentian sage, *Salvia patens* 'Blue Angel'
Hardy geranium, *Geranium himalayense* x *pratense*
  'Johnson's Blue'
Heliotrope, *Heliotropium peruvianum* 'Marine'
Leadwort, *Ceratostigma plumbaginoides*
Monkshood, *Aconitum napellus*
Peach-leaved bellflower, *Campanula persicifolia*
  'Highcliff' (above)
Speedwell, *Veronica austriaca* ssp. *teucrium*
  'Shirley Blue'

Shrubs
Bluebeard, *Caryopteris* x *clandonensis*
  'Heavenly Blue'
California lilac, *Ceanothus* x *delilanus* 'Topaz'

Climbers
Clematis 'Lady Northcliffe'

Cyan Blue

Annuals
Forget-me-not, *Myosotis alpestris*

Perennials
Blue flax, *Linum perenne*
Cupid's dart, *Catananche caerulea*
Fumitory, *Corydalis flexuosa*
Himalayan blue poppy, *Meconopsis betonicifolia*
Honeywort, *Cerinthe major* 'Purpurascens' (above)
Hound's tongue, *Cynoglossum nervosum*
Lithodora diffusa 'Heavenly Blue'
Oxypetalum caeruleum 'Heavenborn'
Stokes' aster, *Stokesia laevis* 'Blue Star'
Woodland sage, *Salvia uliginosa*

Shrubs
Lacecap hydrangea, *Hydrangea macrophylla*
  'Teller Blue'

Climbers
Blue sweet pea, *Lathyrus sativus* 'Azureus'

Green

Annuals
Bells-of-Ireland, *Moluccella laevis*

Perennials
Stinking hellebore, *Helleborus foetidus*

Foliage plants
Butterbur, *Petasites japonicus*
Chameleon plant, *Houttuynia cordata*
Evening primrose, *Oenothera speciosa*
Honesty, *Lunaria rediviva*
Horehound, *Marrubium cylleneum*
Hosta plantaginea
Macleaya microcarpa
Marjoram, *Origanum vulgare*
Meum athamanticum
Navelwort, *Omphalodes cappadocica*
Rhubarb, *Rheum palmatum*
Rodgersia podophylla
Solomon's seal, *Polygonatum odoratum*

Grasses
Bearskin fescue, *Festuca scoparia*
Drooping sedge, *Carex pendula*
Fountain grass, *Pennisetum alopecuroides*
Wood rush, *Luzula nivea*

Ferns
Deer fern, *Blechnum spicant*
Royal fern, *Osmunda regalis*
Wall fern, *Polypodium vulgare*

Lime Green

Shrubs
Bloodflower, *Asclepias curassavica*
Chaste tree, *Vitex agnus-castus*
Cranberry bush, *Viburnum opulus* 'Xanthocarpum'
Golden curls willow, *Salix* 'Erythroflexuosa'
Hornbeam, *Carpinus betulus*
Japanese flowering cherry, *Prunus serrulata*
Mock orange, *Philadelphus coronaries* 'Natchez'

Climbers
Boston ivy, *Ampelopsis tricuspidata*,
    A. brevipedunculata
Chocolate vine, *Akebia quinata*
Crimson glory vine, *Vitis coignetiae*
Dutchman's pipe, *Aristolochia durior*
Japanese hydrangea vine, *Schizophragma*
    hydrangeoides

Annuals
Flowering tobacco, *Nicotiana* 'Havana Green,'
    'Lime Green,' 'Nicki Lime'
Thoroughwax, *Bupleurum rotundifolium* 'Garibaldi'

Bulbs
Sweet potato vine, *Ipomoea batatas* 'Margarita'

Perennials
Hosta 'Royal Standard'
Lady's mantle, *Alchemilla mollis* (above)
Martin's spurge, *Euphorbia martini*
Siberian spurge, *Euphorbia seguieriana* ssp.
    niciciana
Thyme, *Thymus* x *citriodorus* 'Golden Darf'
Wood spurge, *Euphorbia amygdaloides* var. *robbiae*

Foliage plants
Burning bush, *Kochia trichophylla, K. Scoparia*
Coral bells, *Heuchera* 'Key Lime Pie'
Heucherella 'Gold Strike'
Hosta 'Lunar Eclipse'
Sedum 'Lemon Ball'

Grasses
Millet grass, *Milium effusum* 'Aureum'

Shrubs
Black locust, *Robinia pseudoacacia* 'Frisia'
Bridal wreath, *Spiraea japonica* 'Goldmound'
Dogwood, *Cornus alba* 'Aurea'
European beech, *Fagus sylvatica* 'Darwyck Gold'
Golden box honeysuckle, *Lonicera nitida*
    'Baggesen's Gold'
Golden full moon maple, *Acer shirasawanum*
    'Aureum'
Honey locust, *Gleditsia triacanthos* 'Sunburst'
Japanese barberry, *Berberis thunbergii* 'Gold Torch'
Mexican orange, *Choisya ternate* 'Sundance'

Climbers
Golden hop vine, *Humulus lupulus* 'Aureus'

The Pastel Colors

Primrose

Annuals
African marigold, *Tagetes erecta* 'Eskimo'
Petunia 'Prism Sunshine'
Sunflower, *Helianthus annuus* 'Valentine'

Bulbs
Tulip, *Tulipa* 'Spring Green' (above)

Perennials
Christmas rose, *Helleborus niger* 'Maxima'
Lavender cotton, *Santolina rosmarinifolia* 'Primrose Gem'
Marguerite daisy, *Chrysanthemum frutescens* 'Butterfly'
Mediterranean spurge, *Euphorbia characias*
Pink, *Dianthus knappii*
Tickseed, *Coreopsis verticillata* 'Moonbeam'
Yarrow, *Achillea millefolium* 'Hoffnung'

Shrubs
Buttercup winter hazel, *Corylopsis pauciflora*
Magnolia 'Elizabeth'

Butter Yellow

Annuals and biennials
Nemesia 'Pineapple'
Slipperwort, *Calceolaria integrifolia*
Yellow foxglove, *Digitalis grandiflora*

Bulbs
Lily, *Lilium* 'Boogie Woogie'

Perennials
African daisy, *Osteospermum* 'Cream'
Cephalaria gigantean
Golden box honeysuckle, *Lonicera nitida* 'Baggesen's Gold'
Golden marguerite, *Anthemis tinctoria* 'E. C. Buxton'
Lupine, *Lupinus* 'Chandelier' (above)
Magnolia 'Yellow Bird'
Marguerite daisy, *Chrysanthemum frutescens* 'Primrose Petite'
Monkshood, *Aconitum vulparia*
Red hot poker, *Kniphofia* 'Little Maid'
Rhododendron 'Betty Robertson,' *R. repens* 'Curlew'
Saxifrage, *Saxifraga* x *elizabethae*
Solidaster luteus
Tickseed, *Coreopsis grandiflora* 'Sunray'
Tufted hair grass, *Deschampsia caespitosa* 'Goldschleier'
Yarrow, *Achillea* 'Coronation Gold'

Climbers
Honeysuckle, *Lonicera japonica* 'Halliana'
Jasmine, *Jasminum nudiflorum*
Lady Banks rose, *Rosa banksiae* 'Lutea'

Apricot

Annuals and biennials
Nasturtium, *Tropaeolum* 'Lady Bird,' 'Apricot Gleam'
Nemesia 'Peach'
Pansy, *Viola* 'Antique Shades'
Pot marigold, *Calendula* 'Bonbon Apricot'
Sea lavender, *Statice sinuate* 'Qis Apricot'
Snapdragon, *Antirrhinum majus* 'Peaches and Cream'
Verbena 'Peaches & Cream'

Bulbs
Dahlia 'Peach,' 'Hindu Star'

Perennials
Bearded iris, *Iris germanica* 'Tangerine Sky'
Cinquefoil, *Potentilla* x *tonguei*
Globeflower, *Trollius* 'Orange Globe'
Mallow, *Malva* 'Fire and Ice'
Mullein, *Verbascum* 'Southern Charm'
Sun rose, *Helianthemum* 'Old Gold'

Shrubs
Knap Hill azalea, *Rhododendron* 'Klondyke'
Rose, *Rosa* 'Vanilla Perfume,' 'Morabito'

Climbers
Rose, *Rosa* 'Crépuscule'

Saffron Orange

Annuals and biennials
California poppy, *Eschscholtzia californica* 'Apricot Chiffon'
Cosmos sulphureus
Everlasting, *Helichrysum bracteatum* 'Flame'
French marigold, *Tagetes patula* 'Durango Tangerine'
Gazania kresbiana 'Solana,' *G. rigens* 'Orange Magic'
Pansy, *Viola* 'Deep Orange'

Bulbs
Canna 'Aranyalom'
Dahlia 'Royal Wedding'
Tulip, *Tulipa* 'Princess Irène'

Perennials
Lotus maculates 'Gold Flash'
Mullein, *Verbascum* 'Helen Johnson'
Orange fleabane, *Erigeron aurantiacus*
Sneezeweed, *Helenium* 'Waldtraut'
Sun rose, *Helianthemum* 'Honeymoon'
Yellow sage, *Lantana camara* 'Sunkiss'

Shrubs
Bloodflower, *Asclepias curassavica*
Knap Hill azalea, *Rhododendron* 'Gibraltar' (above)
Witch hazel, *Hamamelis* x *intermedia* 'Jelena'

Climbers
Black-eyed Susan vine, *Thunbergia alata* 'Orange'
Trumpet creeper, *Campsis* x *tagliabuana* 'Mme Galen'

Porcelain Rose

Annuals
Balsam, *Impatiens balsamina* 'Rose Clair'
Flowering tobacco, *Nicotiana* 'Apple Blossom'
Rose mallow, *Hibiscus moscheutos* 'Rose'
Tree mallow, *Lavatera* 'Pink Beauty'

Bulbs
Dahlia 'Topsy,' 'Shiella Noelle'
Gladiolus 'Orlando'

Perennials
Crimson flag, *Schizostylis coccinea* 'Mrs. Hegaty'
Evening primrose, *Oenothera speciosa*
Fleabane, *Erigeron karvinskianus*
Foamflower, *Tiarella cordifolia* 'Spring Symphony'
Monkshood, *Aconitum napellus* 'Carneum'
New York aster, *Aster novi-belgii* 'Audrey'
Peony, *Paeonia* 'Chalice' (above)
Rose campion, *Lychnis coronaria* 'Oculata'

Foliage plants
Dappled willow, *Salix integra* 'Hakuro Nishiki'

Shrubs
Arrowwood, *Viburnum* x *bodnantense*
Honeysuckle, *Lonicera fragrantissima*
Japanese snowball, *Viburnum plicatum* 'Pink Beauty'
Mophead hydrangea, *Hydrangea macrophylla* 'Mousseline'
Saucer magnolia, *Magnolia* x *soulangiana* 'Brozzonii'
Tree mallow, *Lavatera* 'Barnsley'

Pale Pink

Annuals
Cosmos bipinnatus 'Sonata Pink Blush'
Flowering tobacco, *Nicotiana affinis* 'Avalon Bright Pink' (above)
Spider plant, *Cleome spinosa* 'Cherry Queen'
Zinnia 'Rose'

Bulbs
Ivy-leafed cyclamen, *Cyclamen hederifolium*
Tulip, *Tulipa* 'Angélique'

Perennials
Baby's breath, *Gypsophila paniculata* 'Bristol Fairy'
Bugbane, *Cimicifuga (Actaea) racemosa* 'Pink Spike'
Cheddar pink, *Dianthus gratianopolitanus* 'Eydangeri'
Dittany, *Dictamnus albus*
East Indies aster, *Aster tongolensis* 'Berggarten'
Evening primrose, *Oenothera rosea*
Hardy geranium, *Geranium endressii* 'Wargrave Pink'
Heucherella alba 'Bridget Bloom'
Masterwort, *Astrantia major* 'Rosea'
New York aster, *Aster novi-belgii* 'Fellowship'
Stone cress, *Aethionema armenum* 'Warley Rose'
Twinspur, *Diascia anastrepa*
Wild sweet William, *Phlox maculata* 'Alpha'

Shrubs
Higan cherry, *Prunus subhirtella* 'Autumnalis'
Saucer magnolia, *Magnolia* x *soulangiana*
Tree mallow, *Lavatera* 'Silver Cup'

Climbers
Clematis 'Comtesse Bouchaud,' *C. armandii* 'Apple Blossom'
Japanese wisteria, *Wisteria floribunda* 'Rosea'
Rose, *Rosa* 'New Dawn'
Twining snapdragon, *Asarina scandens* 'Mystic Rose'

Deep Rose

Annuals and biennials
Bedding geranium, *Pelargonium* 'Balcony Rose'
English daisy, *Bellis perennis* 'Carmine'
Nasturtium, *Tropaeolum* 'Cherry Rose'
Nemesia 'Blackberry'
Spider plant, *Cleome spinosa* 'Rose Queen'
Verbena 'Salmon'

Bulbs
Dahlia 'Park Princess'

Perennials
Clary sage, *Salvia sclarea*
Japanese anemone, *Anemone japonica*
   'Rubra Plena'
Knapweed, *Centaurea pulcherrima*
New England aster, *Aster novae-angliae* 'Rosanna'
Obedient plant, *Physostegia virginiana*
   'Bouquet Rose'
Oriental poppy, *Papaver orientale* 'Rosenpokal'
   (above)
Red valerian, *Centranthus ruber*
Wild sweet William, *Phlox maculata* 'Rosalinde'

Shrubs
California lilac, *Ceanothus x pallidus* 'Perle Rose'
Camellia japonica 'Comte de Gomer'
Dwarf Russian almond, *Prunus tenella* 'Firehill'
Mophead hydrangea, *Hydrangea macrophylla*
   'Hamburg'
Rose of Sharon, *Hibiscus syriacus* 'Aphrodite'
Tree mallow, *Lavatera* 'Rosea'

Climbers
Clematis Montana 'Tetrarosa'

Lilac-Pink

Annuals
Bedding geranium, *Pelargonium* 'Horizon Violet'
Chinese aster, *Callistephus chinensis* 'Lilac Rose'
Cuphea 'Lila'
Petunia 'Bourgogne'
Spider plant, *Cleome spinosa* 'Cherry Queen'

Perennials
Dame's rocket, *Hesperis matronalis*
Delphinium 'Astolat,' 'Blue Jay'
Hardy geranium, *Geranium* 'Salome'
Joe Pye weed, *Eupatorium maculatum*
   'Atropurpureum'
Masterwort, *Astrantia major*
Purple coneflower, *Echinacea pallida, E. purpurea*
   (above)
Sea thrift, *Armeria maritima*
Sedum spectabile 'Carmen'
Stars-of-Persia, *Allium christophii*
Twinspur, *Diascia* 'Ruby Field'
Yarrow, *Achillea millefolium* 'Lilac Beauty'

Shrubs
Butterfly bush, *Buddleia alternifolia*
   'Summer Beauty'
Lilac, *Syringa* 'Josee'
Mophead hydrangea, *Hydrangea macrophylla*
   'Ayesha'
Purple rock rose, *Cistus purpureus*
Rhododendron 'Albert Schweitzer'
Tree mallow, *Lavatera* 'Bredon Springs'

Climbers
Clematis 'Proteus'

Lilac

Annuals
Bacopa, *Sutera cordata* 'Blue Showers'
Chinese aster, *Callistephus chinensis* 'Lilac'
Impatiens 'Bahia,' 'Lilac'
Verbena 'Lavender Lace'

Bulbs
Dahlia 'Lilac Time'
Spring starflower, *Ipheion uniflorum*

Perennials
Bearded iris, *Iris germanica* 'Amethyst Flame'
Beard tongue, *Penstemon* 'Sour Grapes'
Bellflower, *Campanula poscharskyana* 'Lisduggan'
Blue hibiscus, *Alyogyne huegelii* 'Santa Cruz'
   (above)
Fringed pink, *Dianthus superbus*
Garden phlox, *Phlox paniculata* 'Progress'
Heath aster, *Aster ericoides* 'Ringdove'
Hebe 'Youngii'
Lemon thyme, *Thymus serpyllum*
Meadow rue, *Thalictrum delavayi*
Purple-leafed culinary sage, *Salvia officinalis*
   'Purpurascens'
Rock cress, *Aubrieta* 'Blue King'
Woodland phlox, *Phlox divaricata* 'Chattahoochee'

Shrubs
Butterfly bush, *Buddleia alternifolia*
Cutleaf lilac, *Syringa laciniata*
Lilac, *Syringa vulgaris* 'Belle de Nancy'

Climbers
Clematis 'Prince Charles'

Mauve

Annuals
Petunia grandiflora 'Blue'
Stock, *Matthiola incana* 'Blue'

Perennials
Allegheny monkey flower, *Mimulus ringens*
Buenos Aires verbena, *Verbena bonariensis*
Culinary sage, *Salvia officinalis*
Fleabane, *Erigeron* 'Wupertal'
Hosta elata
Pasque flower, *Pulsatilla vulgaris*
Rock cress, *Aubrieta* 'Blue Cascade'
Self-heal, *Prunella x webbiana*

Shrubs
Catawba rhododendron, *Rhododendron*
    catawbiense 'Boursault,' 'Grandiflorum'
Hydrangea aspera var. *villosa*

Climbers
Japanese wisteria, *Wisteria japonica*
    'Violacea Plena'

Plum

Annuals
Swan River daisy, *Brachycome iberidifolia*

Bulbs
Gladiolus 'Velvet Eyes'

Perennials
Bear's breeches, *Acanthus spinosus*
Daylily, *Hemerocallis* 'Chicago Queen'
Oriental poppy, *Papaver orientale* 'Patty's Plum'
Toadshade, *Trillium sessile*
Verbena Canadensis 'Toronto'

Foliage plants
Beef plant, *Iresine herbstii*
Houseleek, *Sempervivum* 'King George'
Painted nettle, *Coleus blumei* 'Juliet Quartermain,'
    'Velvet Red'
Purple spurge, *Euphorbia dulcis* 'Chameleon'
Wood sorrel, *Oxalis* 'Burgundy Wine'

Shrubs
Rose 'Cardinal de Richelieu,' 'Souvenir d'Alphonse
    Lavallée'

Purple Plum

Annuals
Flossflower, *Ageratum* 'Pearl Royal'

Perennials
Beard tongue, *Penstemon* 'Russian River'
Bee balm, *Monarda* 'Prairienacht'
Burnet, *Sanguisorba obtusa*
Columbine, *Aquilegia viridifolia*
False hellebore, *Veratrum nigrum*
Hen-and-chicks, *Sempervivum tectorum*
    'Violaceum'
Live-forever, *Sedum telephium* 'Purpureum'

Foliage plants
Fountain grass, *Pennisetum setaceum* 'Rubrum'
Painted nettle, *Coleus blumei* 'Dark Star'
Sweet potato vine, *Ipomoea batatas* 'Blackie'

Climbers
Chocolate vine, *Akebia quinata*
Sweet pea, *Lathyrus odoratus* 'Cupani's'

Lavender-Blue

Annuals and biennials
Bush violet, *Browallia speciosa* 'Blue Dream'
Edging lobelia, *Lobelia erinus* 'Lavender'
Flossflower, *Ageratum mexicanum* 'Royal Blue'
Petunia 'Heavenly Lavender'

Perennials
Bugloss, *Anchusa azurea* 'Dropmore'
Catmint, *Nepeta* x *faassenii* 'Six Hills Giant,' *N. mussinii*
Delphinium 'Cameliard'
Garden phlox, *Phlox paniculata* 'Eventide'
Meadow sage, *Salvia pratensis haematodes*
Orchid primrose, *Primula vialii*
Peach-leaved bellflower, *Campanula persicifolia* 'Percy Piper'
Pincushion flower, *Scabiosa caucasica* 'Perfecta'
Russian sage, *Perovskia atriplicifolia*
Woodland phlox, *Phlox divaricata*

Shrub
English lavender, *Lavandula angustifolia* (above)

Climber
Clematis 'Lasurstern,' 'Mrs. Hope'

Sky Blue

Annuals and biennials
Bush violet, *Browallia speciosa* 'Ocean Light Blue'
Edging lobelia, *Lobelia erinus* 'Sky Blue'
Flossflower, *Ageratum mexicanum* 'Blue Lagoon'
Forget-me-not, *Myosotis alpestris*
Love-in-a-mist, *Nigella damascena* 'Baby Blue'
Pansy, *Viola* 'Sky Blue'
Petunia 'Surfinia Sky Blue'

Perennials
Adriatic bellflower, *Campanula garganica*
Bearded iris, *Iris germanica* 'Pacific Panorama,' 'Tinkerbell'
Bushy aster, *Aster dumosus* 'Blue Baby'
Columbine, *Aquilegia* 'Blue Star'
Creeping forget-me-not, *Omphalodes verna*
Delphinium 'Summer Sky,' *D.* x *belladonna* 'Cliveden Beauty'
Forget-me-not, *Myosotis palustris*
Heath aster, *Aster ericoides* 'Blue Wonder'
Jacob's ladder, *Polemonium reptans* 'Blue Pearl'
Lily of the Nile, *Agapanthus* 'Blue Triumphator' (above)
Lungwort, *Pulmonaria officinalis* 'Cambridge Blue'
Peach-leafed bellflower, *Campanula persicifolia*
Pitcher sage, *Salvia* azurea
Rock cress, *Aubrieta* 'Blue King'
Speedwell, *Veronica filiformis*

Shrubs
California lilac, *Ceanothus arboreus* 'Trewithen Blue,' *C.* x *delilanus* 'Gloire de Versailles'
Cape leadwort, *Plumbago auriculata* 'Escapade Blue'
Dutch lavender, *Lavandula* x *intermedia*
Rosemary, *Rosmarinus officinalis*
Tree germander, *Teucrium fruticans* 'Azureum'

Climbers
Clematis 'Blue Light,' 'Belle Nantaise'
Morning glory, *Ipomoea purpurea* 'Heavenly Blue'

Blue-Green

Annuals
Verbena 'Pearl'

Perennials
Baby's breath, *Gypsophila repens*
Blue spurge, *Euphorbia myrsinites*
Blue star, *Amsonia tabernaemontana*
Carnation sedge, *Carex panicea*
Columbine, *Aquilegia*
Cottage pink, *Dianthus plumarius*
False dittany, *Ballota pseudodictamnus*
False indigo, *Baptisia australis*
Honey flower, *Melianthus major*
Horned poppy, *Glaucium flavum*
Hosta sieboldiana 'Bressingham Blue,' 'Elegans,'
    H. x *tardiana* 'Halcyon'
Iceland poppy, *Papaver nudicaule*
Lady's mantle, *Alchemilla erythropoda*
Lungwort, *Mertensia maritime*
Macleaya microcarpra
Marguerite daisy, *Chrysanthemum frutescens*
Meadow rue, *Thalictrum aquilegifolium, T. flavum*
    sp. glaucum
Prickly burr, *Acaena magellanica*
Rue, *Ruta graveolens*
Sea holly, *Eryngium amethystinum*
Spurge, *Euphorbia* 'Despina'
Stonecrop, *Sedum cyaneum* 'Rosenteppich,'
    S. sieboldii
Western bleeding heart, *Dicentra formosa*
Willowherb, *Epilobium dodonaei*

Shrubs
Dorycnium hirsutum
Hebe pinguifolia
Scorpian senna, *Coronilla emerus*

Climbers
Clematis recta

Bright Green

Annuals
Flowering tobacco, *Nicotiana* 'Havana Green'
Zinnia 'Envy'

Bulbs
Gladiolus 'Green Star'

Foliage plants
Baby's tears, *Soleirolia soleirolii*
Bleeding heart, *Dicentra spectabilis*
Boneset, *Eupatorium capillifolium* 'Elegant Plume'
False spikenard, *Smilacina racemosa*
Fennel, *Foeniculum vulgare*
Foamflower, *Tiarella cordifolia*
Hebe 'Bowles Hybrid'
Honesty, *Lunaria rediviva*
Hosta plantaginea 'Grandiflora'
Leopard's-bane, *Doronicum orientale*
Pineleaf beard tongue, *Penstemon pinifolius*
Tellima grandiflora
Tickseed, *Coreopsis verticillata*

Grasses
Cypress sedge, *Carex pseudocyperus*

Ferns
Wood fern, *Dryopteris carthusiana*

Shrubs
Box elder, *Acer negundo*
European elder, *Sambucus nigra* 'Madonna'
Hebe 'Pluto'
Indigo, *Indigofera kirilowii*
Japanese barberry, *Berberis thunbergii*
Japanese maple, *Acer palmatum*
Japanese rose, *Kerria japonica*
Lemon verbena, *Aloysia triphylla*
Spike broom, *Cytisus nigricans* 'Cyril'
Spiraea cinerea 'Grefsheim,' *S. thunbergii* 'Jujino
    Pink,' *S.* x *arguta*

White

Pure White

Annuals
Bacopa, *Sutera cordata* 'Snowflake'
Cosmos bipinnatus 'Sonata White'
Statice, *Limonium sinuatum* 'Iceberg'
Tree mallow, *Lavatera trimestris* 'White Miracle'
Zinnia 'Polar Bear'

Bulbs
Crocus 'Jeanne d'Arc'
Dahlia 'Furka,' 'Klondyke,' 'White Perfection'
Hyacinth, *Hyacinthus* 'Carnegie'
Paperwhite, *Narcissus tazetta*
Snowdrop, *Galanthus nivalis*
Tulip, *Tulipa* 'Diana'

Perennials
Balloon flower, *Platycodon grandiflorus* 'Album'
Bugbane, *Cimicifuga (Actaea) simplex* 'White Pearl'
Chamomile, *Anthemis carpatica* 'Karpatenschnee' (above middle)
Coneflower, *Echinacea* 'Kim's Mophead'
Dame's rocket, *Hesperis matronalis* 'Alba Plena'
Delphinium 'Galahad'
Everlasting, *Anaphalis triplinervis*
Foxglove, *Digitalis purpurea* 'Alba'
Garden phlox, *Phlox paniculata* 'Jacqueline Maille'
Gaura, *Gaura lindheimeri*
Hardy geranium, *Geranium clarkei* 'Kashmir White'
Heath aster, *Aster ericoides* 'Monte Casino'
Hosta crispula
Knotweed, *Polygonum weyrichii*
Libertia formosa
Loosestrife, *Lysimachia ephemerum*
Lupine, *Lupinus* 'La Demoiselle'
Masterwort, *Astrantia major* 'Alba'
Ox-eye daisy, *Leucanthemum vulgare* 'May Queen'

Peony, *Paeonia lactiflora* 'Shirley Temple'
Red valerian, *Centranthus ruber* 'Albus'
Summer hyacinth, *Galtonia candicans*
Tussock bellflower, *Campanula carpatica* 'Alba'

Shrubs
Butterfly bush, *Buddleia alternifolia* 'White Profusion'
European elder, *Sambucus nigra*
Lilac, *Syringa vulgaris* 'Comtesse d'Harcourt'
Old-man's-beard, *Chionanthus virginicus*
Pearlbush, *Exochorda x macrantha* 'The Bride'
Peegee hydrangea, *Hydrangea paniculata* 'Unique'
Serviceberry, *Amelanchier lamarckii*
Smooth hydrangea, *Hydrangea arborescens* 'Annabelle'
Star magnolia, *Magnolia stellata*
White forsythia, *Abeliophyllum distichum*
Yulan magnolia, *Magnolia denudata*

Climbers
Chinese wisteria, *Wisteria sinensis* 'Alba'
Clematis 'Marie Boisselot' (above left), *C. armandii*
Climbing hydrangea, *Hydrangea petiolaris*
Japanese wisteria, *Wisteria floribunda* 'Alba'
Silver lace vine, *Polygonum aubertii*

Creamy White

Annuals
African marigold, *Tagetes erecta* 'French Vanilla'
Petunia 'Lime'

Perennials
Goatsbeard, *Aruncus dioicus* 'Glasnevin'
Meadowsweet, *Filipendula ulmaria*
Peony, *Paeonia lactiflora* 'Carrara'
Rodgersia podophylla
Spotted bellflower, *Campanula punctata*
Stonecrop, *Sedum spectabile* 'Stardust'
Sun rose, *Helianthemum* 'Elfenbeinglanz'

Shrubs
Camellia japonica 'Brushfield Yellow,' 'Margaret Davis'
Flowering quince, *Chaenomeles speciosa* 'Kinshden'
Honeysuckle, *Lonicera* 'Winter Beauty'
Knap Hill azalea, *Rhododendron* 'Persil'
Lilac, *Syringa vulgaris* 'Primrose'
Mock orange, *Philadelphus coronaries*
Rhododendron 'Phyllis Korn'
Rose, *Rosa* 'Mme Bravy,' 'Yvonne Barbier,' 'Albéric Barbier'
Rose of Sharon, *Hibiscus syriacus* 'White Chiffon'
Southern magnolia, *Magnolia grandiflora*

Climbers
Clematis 'Henryi'

Gray

Perennials
Alpine marguerite, *Anthemis marschalliana*
Artemisia canescens, *A.* 'Powis Castle'
    A. schmidtiana 'Nana'
Blue fescue, *Festuca glauca*
Blue oat grass, *Helictotrichon sempervirens*
Catmint, *Nepeta x faassenii*
Cinquefoil, *Potentilla atrosanguinea*
Culinary sage, *Salvia officinalis* 'Bergarten'
English lavender, *Lavandula angustifolia*
Everlasting, *Anaphalis triplinervis*
Everlasting, *Helichrysum italicum* ssp. *serotinum*
Gazania pinnata
Greek yarrow, *Achillea ageratifolia*
Groundsel, *Senecio maritima*
Heather, *Calluna vulgaris* 'Silver Knight'
Jerusalem sage, *Phlomis lanata*
Lamb's ear, *Stachys lanata* 'Silver Carpet'
Lavender cotton, *Santolina chamaecyparissus*
Licorice plant, *Helichrysum petiolare*
Miss Wilmott's ghost, *Eryngium giganteum*
Mullein, *Verbascum bombyciferum*
Rose campion, *Lychnis coronaria*
Silverbrush, *Convolvulus cneorum*
Silver sage, *Salvia argentea*
Snow-in-summer, *Cerastium tomentosum*
Southernwood, *Artemisia abrotanum*
Speedwell, *Veronica spicata* ssp. *incana*,
    V. longiflora
Spotted dead nettle, *Lamium maculatum*
    'Beacon Silver'
Stonecrop, *Sedum spathulifolium* 'Cape Blanco'
Sun rose, *Helianthemum* 'The Bride'
Tansy, *Tanacetum densum amanii*
White sage, *Artemisia ludoviciana* 'Silver Queen'
Wormwood, *Artemisia absinthium*

Shrubs
Bluebeard, *Caryopteris x clandonensis*
Butterfly bush, *Buddleia davidii*
Cider gum, *Eucalyptus gunnii*
Cotoneaster franchetii
Hebe pinguifolia
Russian olive, *Elaeagnus angustifolia*
Sallow thorn, *Hippophae rhamnoides*
Tree germander, *Teucrium fruticans* 'Azureum'
Willow-leaved pear, *Pyrus salicifolia*

Black

Annuals and Biennials
Hollyhock, *Alcea rosea* 'Nigra'
Nasturtium, *Tropaeolum* 'Black Velvet'
Opium poppy, *Papaver somniferum* 'Black Peony'
Painted nettle, *Coleus blumei* 'Black Prince'
Pansy, *Viola* 'Black Jack,' 'Halloween'
Violet, *Viola* 'Black Molly'

Bulbs
Dahlia 'Prince Noir'
Tulip, *Tulipa* 'Queen of the Night'

Perennials
Columbine, *Aquilegia* 'Black Barlow'
Coneflower, *Rudbeckia* 'Black Beauty'

Foliage plants
Coral bells, *Heuchera* 'Chocolate Ruffles,'
    H. micrantha 'Palace Purple'
Mondo grass, *Ophiopogon planiscapus*
    'Nigrescens' (above)
White snakeroot, *Eupatorium rugosum* 'Chocolate'

Shrubs
Rose, *Rosa* 'Black Baccara'

Combining Colors Successfully

☀ **The harmonious color marriage.** Combinations of the three primary colors, magenta red, cyan blue, and yellow, offer an unlimited range of shades that can be found not only in the color wheel but in the diverse variety of flowers as well. If you are familiar with the rules that govern these harmonies and tonalities, you will then be able to deftly choose colors and shades that will allow you to create floral compositions of great subtlety and plant combinations that are pleasing to the eye. ■

The Pastel Color Scheme

On the color wheel, certain blends produce an effect that we perceive as either hot or cold. Colors ranging from green to purple red, and passing through the different nuances of blue, produce an effect of coolness. Colors ranging from yellow to carmine red, and including all the shades of orange, evoke a sense of warmth and light. These nuances, of course, influence the atmosphere of their own flower bed, but they also extend the feeling of coolness or warmth to the whole garden. Thus, warm-toned compositions are essential for illuminating a flower bed situated on the north side of a building or in a shaded area of the garden. And inversely, the cooler shades can produce a cool feeling that may come as a much appreciated relief in a border, garden, or terrace inundated with sun. The vibrant colors produce a stronger effect, but you can lessen their intensity by combining them with white. This essentially creates pastel compositions that give a softer, more romantic effect. To create a flower bed with pastel shades, start by using the plants proposed in the—albeit nonexhaustive—list of pastel colors. Remember, however, that these soft tones can appear sickly and fade quickly when they are used in full sun. ■

1. Billows of New England asters rise up next to the tawny plumes of maiden grass (*Miscanthus sinensis*) and oriental fountain grass (*Pennisetum orientale*), and the sparkling pale gold seedheads of tufted hair grass (*Deschampsia caespitosa* 'Goldschleier').

2. The gray foliage of southernwood (*Artemisia abrotanum*) sets off a drift of pastel colors ranging from the cool lilac of *Aster novi-belgii* 'Audrey' to the warmer rose of *Sedum spectabile* 'Carmen' and the bold pink tones of *Aster novi-belgii* 'Fellowship' (at bottom) and obedient plant (*Physostegia virginiana* 'Bouquet Rose').

3. Pastel tones, mixed with some white, create a pleasant and soft atmosphere.

3

2

4

The Single-Color Shading

While pastel plantings combine a range of soft colors with an addition of white, color shadings play with variations on a single color, with tonalities that can range all the way from the most saturated hue to white. In this way, you can create many nuances of shading, from the palest to the most intense, using only one color. When this is done correctly, the effect can be very elegant, but if you use the wrong color, the planting can seem somewhat somber and melancholy. This is especially true of those colors that we call cool, like violet or blue, which fare better when combined with other colors. To use these colors, expand your range to include a few related hues on the color wheel, which will produce an effect somewhat closer to a *camaieu* (see page 30) than a true single-color shading.

You can also integrate a few notes of gray; for the most part, this is accomplished with silver foliage plants, as it is rare to find flowers of this color. Gray is actually a very useful color in any border, because of its chameleon nature. Though it can range from very light to very dark, gray, as a mixture of white and black, is neutral if no other color is placed with it. However, as soon as it is combined with hot colors like red, yellow, or orange, it brings their brightness to life, heightening the effect of a fiery border. On the other hand, mixed with cool shades like violet, blue, or green, it contributes to an icy and austere ambience. ■

1. A color shading combines a multitude of tonalities closely related on the color wheel, ranging from pale to deep; here, rhododendrons and azaleas create a swath of hues ranging from creamy yellow to scarlet.

2. French marigolds (*Tagetes patula* 'Orange' and 'Gold') underline this single-color shading on a yellow theme, adding a deeper counterpoint to the yellow pompom flowers of a double golden marguerite (*Anthemis tinctoria*), pale 'Prism Sunshine' petunias, and lime-shaded flowering tobacco (*Nicotiana* 'Havana Green').

3. Around a foundation of *Petunia grandiflora* 'Blue' and *Brachycome iberidifolia*, this mauve color shading is completed by Buenos Aires verbena (*Verbena bonariensis*), mealycup sage (*Salvia farinacea* 'Blue Bedder'), and a border of flossflower (*Ageratum* 'Pearl Royal'), set off by the silver of dusty miller.

4. The umbels of lily of the Nile (*Agapanthus* 'Blue Umbrella') emerge from a color shading built around violet-plum, brought together by ageratum, *Verbena canadensis* 'Toronto,' and mealycup sage (*Salvia farinacea*).

The *Camaieu*

1. An elegant pink *camaieu* brings together *Sedum spectabile* 'Carmen,' *Verbena bonariensis*, and billows of New England aster.

The secondary colors green, orange, and violet are produced when two of the three primary colors of the color wheel are mixed. The tertiary colors are in turn created by mixing a primary color with a secondary color; red and orange, for example, create orange-red. These twelve bright colors make up the color wheel. The French term *camaieu* describes a composition made up of variations and shades of one color plus one or more closely related colors. Thus, a *camaieu* of red is based on red, but also includes colors that are near it on the color wheel, like purple or orange. To create a successful *camaieu*, it is best to limit yourself to only two colors so as not to create

excessive and gaudy effects. Some combinations should be avoided, as they are difficult to integrate into a garden. This is true of magenta and cyan, for example; combining these intense shades in a border creates a sharp contrast that wearies the eye and is a bit off-putting. To make it a little more harmonious, allow blue shades to dominate. Together, cyan blue and orange-red create a harsh contrast that can be softened by using a higher proportion of blue or adding yellow or violet. Magenta gains nothing juxtaposed to yellow; the contrast is hard on the eye. To temper this combination, make sure that yellow clearly dominates, bridge the gap with orange notes, and scatter silver foliage plants throughout the composition. Mixed with violet-blue, magenta gives a very artificial result that lacks finesse and elegance. To add nuance to this, use a softer pink instead of magenta and reduce the violet or replace it entirely with mauve. Finally, blues and greens, used by themselves, create a cold and often melancholy atmosphere, but you can brighten up the look by scattering a few touches of silver-gray and white. ■

Tips

On the color wheel, every color has an opposite, or complementary, color. This is made by mixing two primary colors. Thus, the complementary color of red is green, made by mixing blue and yellow. The complementary color of blue is orange, created by mixing yellow and magenta. And yellow's complementary color is violet, a mix of cyan and magenta. Complementary colors are essential, as they assure stability and visual equilibrium in a border.

2. In a graceful composition, bearded iris (*Iris germanica* 'Amethyst Flame') rises up from a carpet of *Nepeta* x *faassenii* 'Six Hills Giant' to produce a *camaieu* backed up by the white lupine 'La Demoiselle' and bugloss (*Anchusa azurea* 'Dropmore').

3. Roses 'Florette,' 'Nathalie,' and 'Juana' create a *camaieu* of pinks.

4. Against the tall blades of *Crocosmia* 'Lucifer,' a *camaieu* of cool pink tree mallow (*Lavatera* 'Silver Cup') and clary sage (*Salvia sclarea*) blends with salmon-colored ('Cahuita') and red ('Coral') impatiens.

2

3

4

1. Red valerian (*Centranthus ruber*), the wild form of which has deep pink flowers, is a perennial that self-seeds with generosity. When the white *Centranthus ruber* 'Albus' and the red *Centranthus ruber* 'Coccineus' are hybridized, their many varied shades of pink create a delightful *camaieu*, particularly ravishing with herbaceous peonies.

2. Old roses shaped like opulent perfumed peony blooms in a number of soft colors create elegant borders. To break them up a bit, insert a perennial between every three or four roses to make the overall effect more light and graceful. Here, armfuls of catmint (*Nepeta* x *faassenii*) fill the composition with billows of lavender-blue flowers. Russian sage (*Perovskia atriplicifolia*), *Gaura lindheimerii*, and obedient plant (*Physostegia virginiana*) will produce a similar effect but in different colors.

3. In the summer, fill window boxes or hanging planters with a *camaieu* of purple and pink flowers. Here, the deeper hues of pink bedding geranium (*Pelargonium* 'Balcony Rose'), violet petunia 'Twilight Blue,' and wine-red petunia 'Bourgogne' are discreetly set off by the small white flowers of bacopa (*Sutera cordata* 'Snowflake'), interwoven through the foliage.

3

4

1

2

4. Simple but charming, this lively assembly of perennials brings together the violet plum color of bee balm (*Monarda* 'Prairienacht'), the deep indigo of monkshood (*Aconitum napellus*), and the pale pink of wild sweet William (*Phlox maculata* 'Alpha').

5. To bring out the full glory of color in a *camaieu*, interweave islands of silver-foliaged perennials; here, lamb's ears (*Stachys lanata*) bring together the pink shades of hardy geraniums (*Geranium endressi* 'Wargrave Pink') and cheddar pinks (*Dianthus gratianopolitanus* 'Eydangeri') and the lavender-blue of catmint (*Nepeta mussinii*).

The Monochromatic Color Scheme

Monochromatic groupings bring together plants whose flowers are of the same color, or in a very narrow range of shades. Dark colors are difficult to use here, as the overall effect will be very drab and monotonous. The easiest to use are light colors or white, which is not on the color wheel but is ac- tually the combination of all colors. In the garden, white is used to lighten a group- ing or to soften bright colors. The shades of white vary according to the flower, and the presence of other colors can give a pink or bluish note to a white that seems perfectly pure. At the other extreme, there are really no totally black flowers, though some col- ors, like purple, can be dark enough to ap- pear black. The darkest hues are extremely valuable in lending depth to a border; for this purpose, there are few to match a fo- liage plant like mondo grass (*Ophiopogon planiscapus* 'Nigrescens'). ∎

1. White is most widely used to create monochromatic schemes. Here, the white-edged foliage of *Hosta crispula* rises from a carpet of everlasting (*Anaphalis triplinervis*). The plumes of garden phlox (*Phlox paniculata* 'Jacqueline Maille') alternate with both the fine spikes of loosestrife (*Lysimachia ephemerum*) and the bells of summer hyacinth (*Galtonia candicans*).

2. This composition plays on a yellow theme, from the softest shade in the Knap Hill azalea (*Rhododendron* 'Persil'), with its sand white petals, to the most saturated in the pale apricot blossoms of another Knap Hill hybrid (*Rhododendron* 'Klondyke'), backed up by the clearer yellow of swamp azalea (*Rhododendron viscosum* 'Arpège'), with its delicately perfumed blossoms.

3. In this monochrome, the variegated foliage of *Fuchsia magellanica* 'Aureum' offers a luminous backdrop for daylilies (*Hemerocallis* 'Corky') and slipperwort (*Calceolaria integrifolia*).

2

3

The Cool Color Scheme

Some delightful borders principally rely on a cool pastel color scheme. These begin with shades of blue, which evokes water and thus coolness, but also use a wide range of shades of green, an invigorating color. In a border, be sure not to overdo the use of pastel colors such as very light greens or yellows or pale blue, as they often appear wan and sickly unless they are enhanced by a few notes of brightness, like vermilion, bright yellow, or a stronger green. In addition, don't forget that foliage in itself generally contributes to the cool side of the spectrum in a border, and is all the more important since its color not only mixes with those of the flowers but remains long after the blossoms have faded. There are many shades of green, from those tending toward blue to those on the yellow side. When it has more blue in it, green can appear dark and gloomy; with more yellow, it appears brighter. ■

1. In the shade of an old well house, the deep rose flowers of red valerian (*Centranthus ruber*), the violet spikes of speedwell (*Veronica longiflora* 'Blauriensin'), and the blues of catmint (*Nepeta* x *faassenii*) play off the chartreuse yellow bracts of Mediterranean spurge (*Euphorbia characias*) in a combination both acidic and cool.

1

2

The Opulent Color Scheme

Deep, saturated reds are the dominant motif of rich, opulent environs. On the yellow and orange side of its range, red invokes action, fire, and passion, while red that tends toward the maroons and purples becomes a dramatic hue, suggesting strength and solidity. These are the shades to look for when you want to compose a luxurious scene, which can be accented by scattering a few touches of royal blue and dark green here and there. Don't forget brown and near black, which add a bit of mystery. Watch out, however, that you do not make the composition so dark that it becomes gloomy and oppressive. You can avoid a somber atmosphere, lighten the look of richly colored borders, and set off these lush hues to their best effect with deft touches of yellow and gray: You can't have riches without silver and gold. ∎

1. A range of shades of red give this scene an opulent effect. Here, *Verbena peruviana* and red bedding geraniums (*Pelargonium*) assert themselves all the more strongly against the paler notes of yellow marguerite daisy (*Chrysanthemum frutescens* 'Butterfly') and tree wormwood (*Artemisia arborescens*).

2. To evoke distant lands, combine ocher and oranges. Along the length of this walkway, a border of golden yellow and deep red nasturtiums (*Tropaeolum* 'Vesuvius' and 'Empress of India') sets off armfuls of tawny-hued yarrow (*Achillea* 'Terra Cotta').

The Exotic Color Scheme

Plantings that evoke exotic atmospheres combine the exuberance and density of bright and dark greens with the nonchalance of shades of orange. These warm hues create a feeling of gaiety, bringing to mind hot summer vacations. In spring, they wake up the garden, foreshadowing the return of balmy weather. Mixed with varying shades of green, from the lightest to the darkest, orange becomes radiant and happy. On the other hand, you will need a deft hand to temper these strong shades in a summer border, so that they do not become too exuberant, or even oppressive. To put the finishing touches on an exotic color scheme, throw in a few notes of ocher, beige, and light brown, and even some mauves and lavenders. Don't forget black to heighten contrast, or pure white, which both sets off the subtleties of all these hues and offers a soothing respite to the eye. ∎

3

4

The Passionate Color Scheme

To create depth and lively contrast in a bed, use the deepest and most intense shades of blue. In its lightest shades, blue is synonymous with delicateness, purity, and calm, but as the amount of red is increased, it becomes more passionate and dramatic. In between these two polar opposites, shades of cyan blue, dark blue, and marine blue call to mind the color of the sea or ocean. Hues verging on purple provide a touch of elegance, but they also evoke the night and shadows. To carry the analogy of a spirited ocean and its foam-capped waves one step further, add some shades of gray to the border. Whether silver or charcoal, gray can seem icy and austere juxtaposed with a particularly cold color, but it also reinforces the lively and buoyant feeling of a planting. ■

3. Blues evoke passion and dynamism, as here in these mounds of English lavender (*Lavandula angustifolia* 'Munstead') set off by the immaculate white of the tree mallow (*Lavatera trimestris* 'White Miracle') and ox-eye daisies (*Leucanthemum vulgare* 'May Queen').

4. The browns and beiges of tree bark and the various green shades of leaves evoke a natural atmosphere. Here, among the emerald leaves of perennials, feathery fennel (*Foeniculum vulgare*) and a silvery stand of lamb's ear (*Stachys lanata* 'Silver Carpet') light up the soft, pale tones of the old rose 'Ghislaine de Féligonde'.

The Natural Color Scheme

Natural color schemes take as their foundation the shades found in the bark and foliage of trees. Here, green, which elsewhere merely gives an impression of calm and security, can offer, in its most intense shades, a great serenity—an effect not unlike that of walking down a forest path or out in the country. Brown, from beige to the deepest shade, is a warm color that evokes sturdiness and strength—the color of branches and tree trunks full of life, or those honed for construction or the making of furniture. These sober colors can be relieved with a few notes of dark blue, a reminder of the azure sky that is always found as a backdrop in our gardens. ■

The Romantic Color Scheme

Soft colors are the basis of the romantic garden. This is especially so for pink, from old rose to shades of salmon, which lends a charming poetic feel to garden compositions. Add to these hues soft shades of mauve or touches of plum, which will set off the pastel colors nicely. When combining these colors with white, do not use pure white; instead use white with a yellow tint, in varying shades of cream, sand, or ecru. For the finishing touch, don't forget to add shades of very pale green, like sea green or lime green, which produce joyous and luminous effects juxtaposed with pale yellow. Finally, a few scattered touches of silver and gray will throw the pastels into relief, providing sober and neutral islands in a sea of pale hues. ■

1. Achieve an intensely romantic look with a range of shades of pink, from the old rose of masterwort (*Astrantia maxima*) to the amethyst pink globes of stars-of-Persia (*Allium christophii*), set off with the deep plum bottle-brushes of burnet (*Sanguisorba obtusa*) in the foreground.

Designing and Creating the Garden

✻ To successfully develop a border or a flower garden, we have at our disposal not only a rich palette of colors but the endless diversity of the plant world. Annuals, perennials, bulbs, shrubs, and climbing vines in a multitude of forms can be found in a number of varieties whose bloom times spread out over several months. Not one season need be left out. The art of a successful flower garden design rests both in the handling of colors and in the way plants are combined to provide a continuity of bloom while maintaining the desired overall look. But the arrangement of plants in a border and, above all, the way individual species relate to each other within the design, is vital to the success of the final outcome. In fact, the precise arrangement of plants in a bed, for a long time considered of secondary importance, has today come to the fore. The various techniques of planting—in mass or singly, in waves or lines, patchwork or punctuated—produce innovative and sometimes surprising decorative effects. The end result also takes into account the habits of the plants and the form of their blossoms, which we use not only for their numerous colors but also for their infinite diversity of shape and texture. ▪

Flowering Plants

※ **An infinite array of plants for every garden.** There are an unlimited number of plants to choose from to create a bed and decorate a garden. Some live only one season, others for years; some launch an attack on walls, thanks to their twisting branches, while many species, of all shapes and sizes, hug the ground, each with its own silhouette. The characteristics of plants vary widely, and the number of possible combinations are infinite—a godsend to the gardener, who finds such a bounty of raw material with which to express his artistic talents. ■

Annuals

Annuals, those plants whose life is limited to only one season, generally flower from June to October, then fade away. Some will seed themselves, while others, more sensitive to cold, must be sown in greenhouses and planted out after the last frost. Their decorative possibilities are numerous and spectacular, as they offer themselves extravagantly over their short lives. They come in a number of forms, from groundcovers to shrubs, and are used in borders, gardens, or beds. Mixed into summer flower beds, they can also be used as temporary partners to fill out a mixed or perennial border, or planted in containers for a roof garden. Though greedy for fertilizer and water, they are robust, generous, and easy to grow. ▪

1. A summer flower bed can make use of annuals like scarlet sage (*Salvia splendens* 'Fire Star'), with its red spikes, as well as bulbs—here, scarlet dahlias—and a good number of plants that are perennial in mild climates but tender in colder climates. Some such tender perennials here are the purple-leafed beef plant (*Iresine herbstii*); monkey flower (*Mimulus glutinosus*), with its glowing orange flowers; and abutilon, whose variegated leaves resemble those of a maple.

2. Marigolds, petunias, and flowering tobacco are annuals that need to be sown or purchased by the cartloads at nurseries each spring. Easy to please, they grow rapidly and flower abundantly.

3. Tender perennials are cold-hardy only in semi-tropical climates. Elsewhere, they are considered seasonal plants and used like annuals, with which they are often combined. Here, for example, the tender *Gazania pinnata* blends with the yellow-flowered golden marguerite (*Anthemis tinctoria* 'E. C. Buxton') and fleabane (*Erigeron karvinskianus*), with its small daisy blossoms.

Tender Perennials

Some perennials, originally from mild climates, cannot live through the winter in colder regions without winter protection. Like annuals, they fade away in November, wiped out by the frost. These are exotic or tender perennials, the most widely known of which is the bedding geranium, which is actually in the genus *Pelargonium*. Numerous tender perennials are available, and their limitless shapes and colors easily mix with annuals to create summer plantings. They can live several years if they are over-wintered in a greenhouse or any sunny and moist location sheltered from the frost. ▪

2

3

Spring Bulbs

Bulb plants stockpile reserve nutrients in a fleshy underground organ, which feeds the young shoots and their first foliage at the end of winter. Bulbs that flower in the spring light up beds, pots, or borders, and bulbs like snowdrops and crocus create naturalized drifts that need no upkeep. Other bulbous plants that originated from wild species, like tulips and hyacinths, must spend the summer out of the ground. To allow these improved garden varieties to prepare for their winter hibernating period, their foliage must not be cut down right after they have flowered, so the nutrients can make their way back down into the bulb. Cut the foliage only once it has withered completely, dig up the bulbs, and store them in a crate in a dry, dark place at a temperature between 40° and 43° F. You can then replant them the next autumn.■

2

3

Summer Bulbs

1. Emblems of spring, tulips, rising here from a carpet of forget-me-nots, should be dug up and stored in a cool, dry place during the summer. Only species tulips, such as *Tulipa kaufmanniana*, do well left in place for several years.

2. Spring bulbs announce the arrival of spring, but some varieties of tulips are late to appear, blooming at the end of April or the beginning of May, when other vegetation is well on its way.

3. Above an edging of painted nettle (*Coleus blumei*) hybrids, cream-colored petunia 'Prism Sunshine,' and scarlet begonias towers the standout cactus dahlia 'Scarlet Star,' a long-blooming and generous summer bulb; pure white *Cosmos bipinnatus* 'Sonata White' adds a snowy punctuation mark.

Summer bulbs, which grace borders and seasonal container plantings, are less numerous than spring bulbs, but they make up one of the most floriferous groups of summer. Probably best known are dahlias (which, technically speaking, as with a number of summer bulbs, are actually tubers, but are treated in the same way), but the gardener can also make use of cannas, tuberous begonias, gladioli, oxalis, and lilies. Summer bulbs and tubers are generally planted soon after the last frost, in April in milder climates, in May or June in colder ones. In cold climates, they can also be pre-planted in pots and grown in a greenhouse or cold frame to achieve earlier bloom. When planting them in the garden, keep their ultimate height in mind while placing them, then add the appropriate fertilizer and water them well to encourage them to grow and flower. Many summer bulbs, with their numerous and heavy flowers, need to be staked, especially dahlias. Cut off spent flowers to encourage the plant to divert its energy into producing more; in many cases, this will prolong the bloom time up to autumn. In October, after digging them up and letting the foliage die back completely, you can prepare the bulbs for winter storage. Spread them out on a tray in a cool, dry, and dark place; treat them with a fungicide to protect them against rot; then pack them in peat or damp moss until the following spring. ▪

Tips

Deadhead faded flowers to encourage the formation of new buds or prompt some species, like lupines and delphiniums, to produce a second flower spike. In autumn, let the stems, with their dry russet leaves, remain; their beautiful shape adds interest to the winter garden once they have been covered in frost. You can cut them back in the spring at the same time as turning the soil, adding organic fertilizer, and mulching the bed. Every three or four years, in autumn, you should regenerate many perennials by dividing them; this is a good time to completely reorganize your borders.

Perennials

Perennials return to flower anew every year, so they do not need to be replanted. Some of them (herbaceous perennials) die back to the ground in the winter, but their roots will survive underground and send up new shoots again the following spring. Other species keep their foliage and remain decorative all year long. Perennials are very adaptable and demand little maintenance for optimal effect. It is better to plant them in autumn, from September to November, when the earth, still warm, is more favorable to root development that prepares the plants better for the rigors of winter. Now that so many are available in pots, however, perennials can be planted practically year-round. Buying perennials already in bloom allows you to choose the perfect flower color so you can accurately harmonize all the tones of a composition. It is equally possible to start some perennials from seed, or to increase them by division. This is done by digging up the plant in the spring or autumn and, with a sharp knife or a spade, breaking up the clump of roots into a number of smaller pieces. After planting your perennials, put down a layer of landscaping cloth or mulch in the spring, which will keep down weeds, save watering, and keep the soil moist. ■

1. To create a successful perennial bed, keep in mind the heights and shapes of the various plants. Shorter plants should be placed up front and the taller plants in the back, as here with wild sweet William (*Phlox maculata* 'Rosalinde').

2. The soft pink shades of masterwort (*Astrantia maxima* 'Rosea') and bushy asters (*Aster dumosus* 'Fidelio') are enlivened by the gold of *Rudbeckia fulgida* 'Goldsturm' and tawny heleniums. Behind them, the rose shuttle-cocks of coneflower (*Echinacea pallida*) form a bridge between the misty, pale pink flowers of baby's breath (*Gypsophila paniculata* 'Bristol Fairy') and the taller dense rose-purple panicles of Joe Pye weed (*Eupatorium maculatum* 'Atropurpureum').

1

Shrubs

The numerous branches of flowering shrubs, which reach various heights depending on the species, carry a multitude of flowers and bloom at different times of the year. Whether they are low and spreading, bushy, or treelike, they can be used alone, in groups, or mixed with perennials, annuals, or roses. Most flowering shrubs originate in the wild and tolerate a wide range of conditions, but some that hail from hotter climates are sensitive to frost. These are best used in gardens near the sea or in sheltered places. Others dislike chalky earth and will thrive only in acidic soils with plenty of humus in the form of decayed roots, branches, and leaves. These peat-loving plants, which include azaleas, rhododendrons, and camellias, usually prefer part or full shade and produce spectacular spring blossoms. To refine the effect of shrub borders, don't forget to combine flowering shrubs with colorful foliage plants and evergreens. By creating a framework of foliage, these highlight the intensity of flowers and form a green backdrop the whole season. ■

1

1. In earliest spring, Loebner magnolia (*Magnolia x loebneri*) and star magnolia (*Magnolia stellata*) are covered in white flowers before their leaves even bud out. Behind them can be seen the rosy blossoms of saucer magnolia (*Magnolia soulangeana*).

2. The creamy umbels of a European elder (*Sambucus nigra*) and the silver foliage of a Russian olive (*Elaeagnus angustifolia*) rise above a butterfly bush (*Buddleia alternifolia*), with its arching lilac inflorescences, and the rich pink blossoms of *Rhododendron* 'Albert Schweitzer'.

Roses

There are numerous types of roses, including the bush roses, which have single flowers or small flowers collected into clumps called either floribundas or polyanthas. Between three and five feet in height, these are suitable for use in beds, edgings, and borders. Roses are called rebloomers when they bloom more or less continually from spring to autumn; those that produce only one flush of flowers, most often in June, are called once-blooming. Shrub roses include old roses, cultivated at least as far back as the Middle Ages, and modern cultivars created by rose breeders who have tried to recapture the look and fragrance of the roses of bygone days. Reaching a height of up to five feet, they can have a spread of ten to fifteen feet. Shrub roses can have single or double flowers, which are often fragrant; some bloom once, from May to June, while some rebloom up until the fall. They can be used alone or in beds; mixing them with shrubs, perennials, or annuals often adds to their decorative charm, however. To prune bush roses and polyanthas, select the most vigorous canes and cut them below the third bud from the graft. Reblooming shrub roses need only a light pruning in March. For the once-blooming old roses, cut out the old canes every two years so as to thin the crown, and cut back all the canes two feet from the ground every three or four years. ■

3. Roses offer a multitude of habits, like shrub roses and climbers, which need support for their branches.

4. The old shrub rose 'Charles de Mills,' with its lilac-pink blossoms, is a vigorous grower that takes up more space than a bush rose. It is best used at the back of the border, as here, where it sprawls against other roses, like the graceful climber 'New Dawn' with its pale pink flowers.

5. Low-growing polyanthas and standard roses complement each other in their respective habits; the polyanthas offer a foundation that the standard roses rise above like miniature trees.

3

4

5

Climbers

Climbers are shrubs with long, flexible branches that need a support to grow on. Some, like ivy, grapevines, and climbing roses, attach themselves with clingy tendrils, suckers, and even thorns. Others twine their stems around their support, like wisteria, honeysuckle, and knotgrass. Creepers can have decorative flowers or berries and may be deciduous or evergreen. The climbing plants include perennials and tender plants. For spring flowering, choose a Chinese (*Wisteria chinensis*) or Japanese (*Wisteria floribunda*) wisteria or *Clematis Montana* and its varieties. For the summer, opt for the clematis hybrids, trumpet creeper (*Campsis*), silver lace vine (*Polygonum aubertii*), climbing hydrangea (*Hydrangea petiolaris*), honeysuckle, and the innumerable varieties of climbing roses. Annual climbers are those that live only one season. These include nasturtiums (*Tropaeolum*), morning glories (*Ipomoea*), and sweet peas (*Lathyrus odoratus*). Finally, tender climbers like leadwort (*Plumbago*), jasmine (*Jasminum officinale*), bougainvillea, and passionflower dislike frost. They cannot survive the winter in climates with harsh winters unless they are given protection. ■

1. Among the climbing plants, Japanese wisteria (*Wisteria floribunda* 'Alba'), dripping with innumerable panicles of fragrant white flowers, is certainly one of the most spectacular species.

2. Climbing and rambling roses can be vigorous climbers, reaching a height, depending on the variety, of eighteen to thirty feet.

Tips

Climbers need a support for their stems. Decorative structures like pergolas, arbors, arches, or trellises not only act as supports but also create elegant ornaments in the garden. These structures are sold as ready-to-install kits or can be built from scratch with a little know-how. Often, however, climbers are used to decorate a wall or a facade: Simple strands of wire against a wall will be enough to support them.

A Garden for Every Season

✳️ **Twelve months of bloom.** Creating a flower garden is not only about combining plants and shrubs with colors that go well together in a bed. It includes the patient work of spacing out the bloom times to obtain a satisfying floral display throughout the whole year. Although there may not be as many winter bloomers to choose from as plants that flower in the spring and summer, there are still quite enough to brighten the colder months. These are especially precious to the gardener, forming a delicate liaison between autumn and the return of the beautiful days of spring. ■

Spring

Spring-flowering bulbs such as tulips (facing page), like biennials, are the first heralds of the return of the giddy days of spring. These plants wait only for the end of winter to flower. Their buds and flowers are already under way the previous autumn, during what is known as the vegetative phase, when the plants' roots and foliage develop and save up nutrients so that the plant will be prepared to bloom the following spring. Mix bulbs and biennials with ornamental shrubs, perennials, and spring-flowering climbers. Their radiant hues build up in a crescendo from February to June, beginning early spring with soft, pale shades and building up to a brilliant burst of color at the season's peak.

Summer

This is probably the most bountiful season in the flower garden; every kind of flower joins the chorus, from shrubs to roses, perennials, climbers, and bulbs, as well as the prolific annuals, the incontestable queens of summer. The profusion of summer's forms and colors makes choosing difficult. But this diversity makes for limitless combinations; any errors in judgment the overenthusiastic gardener might make easily blend into the crowd. Thus, summer beds (below) are perfect for experimenting with new combinations of flowers and foliage.

Autumn

At the end of summer the garden often falls into a dead zone, as summer bloomers fade before the autumn stars have gotten under way. This can be avoided by selecting summer shrubs, perennials, and especially reblooming roses that extend their bloom longer into the fall season, carrying the border until the autumn flowers arrive. To keep the show up late into the season, be sure to include perennials, particularly asters (below), which come in many varieties that bloom right up to the brink of winter. These spread to fill the spaces left in beds by shrubs, roses, and annuals that have died back. Don't forget to combine them with decorative and colorful foliage plants, like the graceful ornamental grasses that illuminate gardens with gold and red in the month of November. All of these, along with the branches and dead leaves of some perennials, remain of interest well into the winter, their frost-encrusted forms creating fantastic tableaus.

Winter

Though the darkest of all the seasons, winter is not necessarily the most melancholy, nor entirely devoid of flowers. Some shrubs and perennials brave the rigors of winter to offer their graceful blossoms. Though they may be less spectacular than the flamboyant blooms of spring, they are all the more appreciated for their rarity and

delicacy. Think, for example, of witch hazel (*Hamamelis mollis*), Higan cherry (*Prunus subhirtella* 'Autumnalis,' below), *Camellia sasanqua*, and laurastinus (*Viburnum tinus*). Some species, like arrowwood (*Viburnum* x *bodnantense*), holly grape (*Mahonia aquifolium* and *M. bealei*), honeysuckle (*Lonicera fragrantissima*),

and oleaster (*Elaeagnus* x *ebbingei*), not only brighten up the garden but also produce a delicate fragrance. Don't prune these shrubs in the winter until they have finished flowering. Think also of covering your beds with winter heath and hardy bulbs like snowdrops, muscaris, scillas, and winter aconite (*Eranthis*

hyemalis), and punctuate them with a few hellebores, both the Lenten rose (*Helleborus orientalis*) and Christmas rose (*Helleborus niger*), especially near windows, pathways to and from the house, doorways, and terraces.

Planting Styles

The art of arranging plants. If the choice of colors is important in creating a flower border, the way the plants are set out is equally so. It is not a question of setting them in the ground correctly, which is easy enough, but of arranging them in such a way that they work together effectively as a whole. There are a multitude of techniques, and the one you choose will make a great difference to your end result; a border that combines many single plants of different kinds has an entirely different effect from one that uses a large number of the same plant in a solid mass. The whole art of arrangement, then, consists of the way you mix plant species and varieties to create a specific style and effect. ■

Contrasts

To handle your color schemes well and underline a specific mood or style in a garden, it is necessary to create contrasts. In creating a flower border, there are two concerns: the contrast of flower and foliage colors and the contrast of plant and blossom forms. A good way to keep the equilibrium of the whole border is to insert a color note opposite to the dominant color now and then: Red is the opposite of green, orange of blue, and yellow of violet. It is also a good idea to use a few cool colors in a predominately warm scheme, and vice versa, to ensure that the border has some perspective and depth. Just a few touches of blue, for example, will give depth to a bed of yellow flowers. In the same way, it is a good idea to add a darker note to a composition of pale hues; for example, some touches of deep violet leave an imprint of rhythm in a swath of pink. The shapes and styles of the flowers themselves are just as important as their colors. These can most simply be divided into those of large single flowers and those with clusters of smaller blooms. These groups can in turn be divided into plants with round, globular blooms or umbels of many flowers that create flattened forms or perfect spheres, plants with spikes composed of slender flowers, plants that form bouquets of innumerable small flowers, producing a misty and light effect . . . the variety is endless. The art of creating contrasts consists of playing these different types against each other to make the most of each flower and plant form. ■

1

1. To create contrasts in form, bring together different flower shapes. Here, the dense spikes of *Delphinium* 'Blue Bird' serve as a transition between the white globes of the peony (*Paeonia lactiflora* 'Shirley Temple') and the feathery intense red panicles of *Astilbe arendsii* 'Etna'.

2. Colors that are opposite each other on the color wheel produce strong contrasts; here the creamy yellow of yarrow (*Achillea millefolium* 'Hoffnung') sets off the deep violet spikes of woodland sage (*Salvia nemorosa* 'May Night').

3. Mixing hot and cold colors also creates a lively contrast, as in this blue carpet of love-in-a-mist (*Nigella damascena*), pierced by the lemon yellow spikes of tree lupine (*Lupinus arboreus*).

2

3

The Tapestry Garden

This lively mixture of species and varieties creates a riot of colors and forms. Annuals often make up the foundation of this style of planting, but perennials, bulbs, and even vegetables, grasses, and exotic species can also be used. First choose five to nine plants whose colors, flower shapes, and overall habits together create a desired decorative effect. To weave your flower tapestry, set your plants out in a succession of rows according to a sequence that you determine beforehand to create the most interesting balance and contrast among the plants. Repeat this sequence in the same order throughout the planting, and with the same amount of space between all of the plants, usually about twelve to fifteen inches in every direction, as if planting on a grid. This method creates various strata of plants; the effect of an interwoven tapestry is highlighted by the varied heights, leaf textures, flower shapes, and other characteristics of the different plants. ■

1. Combined in a garden tapestry, the sea green spikes of anise hyssop (*Agastache rugosa* 'Alabaster') that has finished blooming emerge from a fine mist of baby's breath (*Gypsophila paniculata*) against a backdrop of cream-white plumes of knotweed (*Polygonum weyrichii*) and the rich purple flower heads of Joe Pye weed (*Eupatorium maculatum* 'Atropurpureum').

2. This extravagant riot of colors and flower forms results from a combination of perennials: from a foundation of yellow tickseed (*Coreopsis grandiflora* 'Early Sunrise') burst the spikes of deep violet *Delphinium* 'King Arthur' and wine-red beard tongue (*Penstemon* 'Port Wine').

Tips

To create a well-balanced tapestry composition, alternate compact shapes with those that are more slender and airy. The first will make up the foundation of the composition, while the second reach up toward the sky, making their way through the foliage of those below. During the growing season, add stakes or hoops to support bigger plants so that they don't flop over and crush the smaller ones, and prop up heavy flowers that have a tendency to droop after a rain or watering.

1

The Classic Herbaceous Border

In the traditional mixed or herbaceous border, popularized by English garden designers like Gertrude Jekyll, plants are arranged according to height, smallest at the front, building to the tallest at the rear. This crescendo effect gives each plant enough light and space to grow well and allows an uninterrupted view of all. Such a planting style easily forms a harmonious ensemble. Always begin by planting the largest plants as a backdrop to the bed, making sure to leave plenty of room in front of them for the lower varieties. Continue planting the middle zone of the bed, and end in the front with the lowest plants closest to the edge. It is also a good idea to arrange plants in clusters of three or five plants of the same variety; always use an odd number, as asymmetrical groupings give a more natural look to your design. Don't forget to add a little movement by inserting a few taller plants toward the front, or those with flowering spikes that can rise above the lower mass of flowers. ■

1. Inspired by the principle of graduating plant heights from front to back, this border obtains a rhythmic effect from grouping a number of plants of the same cultivar in islands, which produce round shapes that are repeated regularly. Here, lavender and marguerite daisies (*Chrysanthemum frutescens*) form cushions of silver foliage and white flowers overtaken, in the back, by the lime green foliage of Mexican orange (*Choisya ternate* 'Sundance'), which is in turn punctuated by the brilliant red flowers of avens (*Geum chiloense* 'Mrs. Bradshaw').

2. A classic graduated herbaceous border combining many forms and colors, starting with a carpet of stone cress (*Aethionema armenum* 'Warley Rose'), from which thrust the purple stalks of culinary sage (*Salvia officinalis*) and the delicate white blooms of hardy geranium (*Geranium clarkei* 'Kashmir White'). Farther back, ornamental shrubs, among them cranberry bush (*Viburnum opulus* 'Roseum'), complete the crescendo of colors.

The "New Wave" Garden

The "New Wave" style of planting, pioneered by Dutch garden designer Piet Oudolf, draws its inspiration from the horizontal brushstrokes of a painting. Oudolf and his followers base their trademark style on vast and massive undulations, composed of large groups of flowering or colorful foliage plants. Wave plantings are essentially made up of perennials, annuals, and grasses; shrubs and roses are rarely used in this style. Groupings of plants, whether in the form of islands, more or less regular rows, or large swaths, play against each other to produce a bold overall effect. Each section is composed of a single plant variety, selected for flower shape or color or the texture or hue of its foliage. The wave garden's undulating look is to a great extent due to the use of perennials whose supple leaves, whether broad or finely serrated, verdant or silvery, sway in the wind. This effect can also be created by using ornamental grasses, whose stalks and seed heads not only take on a tousled and fluid appearance as they rustle in the breeze but also create a transparent scrim through which the forms of other plants are glimpsed intriguingly. This innovative style, mixing nature and architecture, creates various looks depending on which plants are used, but always gives a wonderful impression of controlled freedom. ■

1. Emerging from a rusty sea of live-forever (*Sedum telephium* 'Purpureum'), the misty blossoms of heath aster (*Aster ericoides* 'Ring Dove') arch like a breaking wave, backed up by the scarlet bottlebrushes of mountain fleece (*Persicaria amplexicaule* 'Atropurpureum').

2. Wine-red mountain fleece and purple loosestrife (*Lythrum virgatum* 'Rose Queen') swaying along with swaths of ornamental grasses illustrate one of the hottest trends in flower gardens today.

Tips

To create your own "New Wave" garden, group fifteen to twenty plants of the same kind together in meandering bands and narrow swaths you have previously outlined on the earth of the border. Use species of different heights, but don't attempt to arrange them according to their height; instead, set groups next to each other in a way that makes the most of the differing texture of their foliage, their habits, and the color of their flowers. After a few years, the most invasive species will tend to overwhelm their neighbors. It will be necessary to use a spade to cut back the conquering tides and regain the clean-edged design that is a hallmark of the style of planting in waves.

The Row Garden

This style of planting gets its inspiration from the "New Wave" planting style, but here the plants are laid out in perfectly straight rows, not meandering streams and islands. Though very contemporary in look, row planting can be used for all styles of gardens. The basic idea is to draw straight lines, either parallel or perpendicular, along a bed, more or less two feet apart. Planting rows set on the diagonal also produces a spectacular effect, but it is only possible when the border is large enough. To give this impression of mass and rhythm, use at least eight to twelve plants of the same species in a row, or you will end up with more of a garden tapestry than a true row garden. Alternate heights and shapes to successfully create an effect of movement between one row and the next as well as to give the overall effect of transparence. For this, it is best to use plants with tall, rigid stems and an airy habit. Keep a strict eye on the orderliness of the rows; the more vigorous species will have a tendency to

get out of hand. When this happens, simply take a spade and cut out the roots and stems that are getting out of line. ■

1. Often, row plantings do not require support with stakes, as varieties with stiff stems tend to support those that might flop or sprawl.

2. Pink hardy geraniums (*Geranium psilostemon* 'Bressingham Flair') alternate with wine red masterwort (*Astrantia*

maxima 'Rubra') and the varied blues of *Delphinium* 'Blue Jay' and 'Blue Bird.'

3. *Solidaster luteus* and the taller gold daisies of *Buphthalmum salicifolium* make a glowing backdrop for a scrim of purple Allegheny monkey flower (*Mimulus ringens*).

4. Row plantings make the most of varying plant heights. Here, *Hemerocallis* hybrids 'Corky' and 'Burning Daylight' shine through tall rose-purple prairie mallow (*Sidalcea malviflora* 'Interlaken'), the somber spikes of bear's breeches (*Acanthus spinosus*), and white ox-eye

daisies (*Leucanthemum vulgare* 'May Queen').

2

3

4

A Notebook of Design Ideas

❋ You've come to a decision; you are going to add color to your garden. Like a painter with his palette and brushes, you will add dabs of different hues to your beds, along your walkways, or around your house. The big difference is, since you are using living plants instead of gouache, you will have to wait a few months to appreciate the result of your creations. So before you begin, take the time to choose the colors that you want to use, and make sure that they not only harmonize among themselves but also work with the surrounding landscape and the facade of your house. Also, keep an eye on how the colors of the flowers work with the foliage of the different plants. Then, select the planting style that will give you the effect that you desire. To help you in orchestrating the bloom of your flower garden, from the garden entrance to your most private retreat, these valuable tips will guide your steps. In every case, proceed in small steps, giving yourself time to judge the effect of your compositions and having the patience to adjust and rework your design endlessly. Unlike a painting, plants grow, and the garden never ceases to evolve. ■

The Welcoming Garden

❋ **Color makes an entrance.** Adorning the area around a garden gate, a doorway, or a stoop with flowers is a gracious, elegant way to greet guests. From seasonally blooming perennials and annuals to shrubs, roses, or climbers, a vast array of plants can be used to create a colorful and attractive entrance. The real art is in not only combining them well but also orchestrating your planting so that something is in bloom from spring to winter without a break, since these areas are used year-round. ▪

The Garden Gate

The area around a garden gate or entrance is inevitably where visitors will pause. Before exploring the garden, guests will ring the bell or call out to announce themselves, then may wait a while at the entrance to be invited in. While they are waiting, they have time to take in, often in some detail, the area around the entrance—an interesting paving material, some novel plant combinations, and so on. So, it is important to take particular care in designing your plantings around doorways. As long as you are careful to leave enough space for the guests to enter easily, you can plant flowers lavishly for a festive, inviting atmosphere. Reserve this space for perennials, annuals, and bulbs, which can be backed by shrubs or climbers to twine around the doorway. The note of color and fragrance this island of flowers brings will envelop guests in an atmosphere of hospitality even before they enter the garden. If the entrance is completely covered in paving that makes any plantings in the ground impossible, create a container garden that allows you to adapt the composition according to the seasons and modify it, when needed. Give priority to perennials, shrubs, and reblooming roses that can stay in place several years in a row and need less care. Don't forget to light up the garden threshold with the winter flowers of hellebores, primroses, and early bulbs. ■

1. This discreet entrance is almost hidden behind a mass of *Crocosmia* 'Emily Mackenzie' and yellow ox-eye daisy (*Buphthalmum salicifolium*), from which rise the stalks of yellow and orange *Kniphofia* cultivars 'Butter Cup' and 'Little Elf' and the angular stems of purple *Verbena bonariensis*.

2. Luminous yellows light up the pathway to a gate. The diaphanous lime green flowers of lady's mantle (*Alchemilla mollis*) spill out of containers on both sides of this walk, backed up by mounds of elecampane (*Inula helenium*) with its yellow daisies, the golden spikes of garden loosestrife (*Lysimachia punctata*), and the silver bracts of sea holly (*Eryngium giganteum*).

2

Tips

The limited dimensions of a garden don't always allow grand flower borders that stretch out forever. Remember, though, that a few carefully chosen and strategically placed plants are enough to create the feeling of a bounty of flowers. Stand at the entrance of your property and look along the paths to your house, looking for the field of vision you naturally scan and the main points of interest and intersections that draw the eye. These are the areas, well in view, where you will want to add a splash of color by arranging a few nice containers filled with flowers.

The Doorway

The front steps or porch and doorway of a residence are the first thing most people look at when they enter someone's property. The architecture of the house, the dimensions and style of the door and windows, as well as the layout of the path to the entrance—all play their part in leading us to the front door. By surrounding the entrance with flowering plants, you add a number of colorful signals that highlight both the doorway and the route to follow to reach it. On the other hand, masses of luxurious vegetation spilling over onto the path can get in the way and even conceal the door, making access to the house more mysterious and difficult. A good solution is to surround the entrance with plants in colors that will show up well against the house's facade and window and door trim. ■

1. Set off by the snowy white flowers of *Exochorda micrantha* 'The Bride,' forget-me-nots (*Myosotis alpestris*), tulips, dwarf rhododendrons, and azaleas announce the return of spring with their soft and fresh colors.

2. A virorous Lady Banks rose (*Rosa banksiae* 'Lutea'), with its multitude of small, pale yellow flowers, arches over a door above a planting anchored by purple rock rose (*Cistus purpureus*) and the pale pink of East Indies aster (*Aster tongolensis* 'Berggarten').

3. Almost encasing this entryway with flowers, a long border accommodates a jumble of plants chosen for their shades of blue and white, like the rose 'Fée des Neiges,' English lavender (*Lavandula angustifolia* 'Hidcote'), and white statice (*Limonium sinuate* 'Iceberg'). Garden phlox (*Phlox paniculata* 'Progress') contributes a brighter touch of rose.

4. The stone stairs that climb up to this house are surrounded by colorful and evergreen shrubs like *Pittosporum tenuifolia* 'Saundersii,' with its elegant clear green leaves outlined in white, box hedge pruned into a ball, and a standard kumquat. Below these, pale pink *Verbena* 'Peaches and Cream' and African daisy (*Osteospermum* 'Mirach') produce cascades of flowers, which are in turn set off by pink and white mounds of marguerite daisies (*Chrysanthemum frutescens*).

5. Lily of the Nile (*Agapanthus*)—a tender perennial that can only survive planted out in the garden like this in a mild climate—and ivy-leafed geranium (*Pelargonium*) smother the entrance to this small house with blue and pink flowers.

2

3

4

5

The House Front

1. The luscious pale pink globes of old roses mixed with clematis give the facade of this house a romantic look, enhanced at ground level by the white bells of foxglove (*Digitalis purpurea* 'Alba') and the rich rose clusters of everlasting pea (*Lathyrus latifolius*).

2. On either side of the door, royal fern (*Osmunda regalis*) and ostrich fern (*Matteuccia struthiopteris*) set a tone of exotic elegance. Varied shades of emerald green set off the white flowers of climbing hydrangea (*Hydrangea petiolaris*) and a creeping rose trained along the wall under the eaves.

To soften a facade and make it more welcoming, it may be enough to plant some climbers and give them free rein to scale the walls of the house. This solution has a certain romantic appeal; however, it is not without its drawbacks. When the house's walls are old and perhaps a bit dilapidated, a lush blanket of leaves and flowers will conceal the imperfections and lend, at relatively little cost, an attractive look to the facade. On the other hand, you may well be reluctant to cover a new or painstakingly restored facade with climbing plants. Whatever the state of repair of the house, the proportions and architectural style of the facade should ultimately be the deciding factor as to whether to cover the walls with climbers. If your house's facade is well-proportioned, with harmoniously placed and distributed windows and doors, it is not really necessary to gild the lily with a mass of greenery that risks overloading,

rather than embellishing, the overall effect. However, there is nothing to stop you from using climbing plants along the base of the walls to form a link between the house and the gardens, or adorning the entranceway with an arching garland of flowers, or even tracing an edging of green between two stories of the house. Climbing plants can be trained against the house on a simple wire stretched tight between two fasteners, along which the vine stretches to create a single green cordon. A curtain of greenery over a large section of a facade can be an invaluable tool when the awkward or irregular placement of windows and doors unbalances the overall effect of the building, or when a house is out of scale, too imposing to harmonize with the garden. Letting vines cover vertical surfaces gives an impression of unity, conceals flaws, and softens the presence of an overwhelming house. To harmoniously distribute ▪ ▪ ▪

• • •

the greenery, you will want to install wooden trellises that, while also being an element of the decor themselves, offer a support on which to train and attach climbers. In selecting the plant varieties that will best adapt to your house, remember that all climbing plants need some kind of support, with the exception of ivy and Virginia creeper, which use suckers or clingy roots to gain a toehold on a wall. When choosing flower colors, think about how they will look against walls, shutters, and the trim of the house. On one hand, you don't want flower colors that clash with the house; on the other, you don't want their shade to be so similar that they disappear against paint or brickwork. Instead, establish a color scheme by selecting one color, or several complementary hues, with which you can compose a *camaieu* or color shading. Finally, don't forget to take advantage of the numerous shades of green in climbing plants' foliage, which can form a lush backdrop and soften the contrast between the facade and the flowers against it. ■

Tips

To enliven your facade for as long a period as possible, mix two different species, such as a climbing rose and a clematis or a honeysuckle, with two distinct seasons of bloom. For an extra punch, you can also use climbing annuals to create a surprise flowering during the summer that you can repeat or change the following year. Among others, morning glories, black-eyed Susans, and sweet peas are easy to grow from seed, demand little maintenance, and need no additional support, as they will use the branches of other plants to climb.

1. Paper flower (*Bougainvillea glabra*) is a tender climber that reaches its full glory only in mild climates. Here, planted in the ground, it raises its prickly branches as far as the balcony. At its feet flourish the glowing flower clusters of yellow sage (*Lantana camara*), a Mediterranean shrub that, if it is not spreading freely in a border, will allow itself to be trained easily against a south-facing wall. In cold climates, these plants should be grown in pots so that they can be brought inside and protected from frost in winter.

2. Reblooming climbing roses are the best shrubby climbers to train along a facade. Don't hesitate to mix them with clematis, morning glories, or—as here—golden hop vine (*Humulus lupulus* 'Aureus').

3. Trained along a network of cables fixed by pitons onto the facade of the house, the flexible canes of climbing roses 'Albertine' and 'City of York' mix with those of Virginia creeper, whose emerald green foliage makes a dense backdrop for their pink and white blossoms.

4. The rose 'Sanders White' covers itself in a multitude of small cream-white flowers, their clusters mingling here with the fragrant yellow flowers of honeysuckle (*Lonicera japonica* 'Halliana').

2

3

4

Around the Windows

The best way to make a facade welcoming is by surrounding its windows with flowers. To this end, shrubs and perennials can be planted next to windows on the ground floor; upper windows can be ornamented with window boxes and hanging baskets of flowers. Flower beds placed just in front of ground-floor windows can be filled with perennials or annuals tall enough to be appreciated from the inside as well. Here, shrubs are generally a poor choice, as they can become too large and begin to interfere with shutters and obscure the view. The stems of some shrubs, however, can be bent and trained like the branches of a climber. This is the case with California lilac (*Ceanothus*), camellias, and burning bush (*Kochia*). You can also install window boxes on windowsills or on ledges attached to the wall below. These decorations can be appreciated both from the interior of the house, where they offer a floral transition to the surrounding landscape, and from outside, where their color animates the facade

by complementing the characteristics of the regional architecture. For these container plantings, you can choose among annuals, bulbs, or perennials of short stature, like rock garden plants and alpines. But don't leave out the possibility of aromatic herbs or even small shrubs or miniature roses. ■

1. Lady Banks' rose (*Rosa banksiae*) and California lilac (*Ceanothus impressus*) create a beautiful flowery screen in front of the window but prevent the shutters from being used.

2. Snow-in-summer (*Cerastium tomentosum*), lavender cotton (*Santolina chamaecyparissus*), with its primrose yellow buttons, and garden pinks (*Dianthus*) weave a carpet of silver at the feet of purple-leafed culinary sage (*Salvia officinalis* 'Purpurascens') and the rose 'Fée des Neiges'—a tableau equally visible from the house and the garden.

Garden Ornament and Furniture

✺ **Touches of color to enliven outdoor rooms.** The places where we spend the most time in the garden, such as terraces bordering the house and sitting areas situated in the garden itself, merit particular attention. Great care should be taken when creating these outdoor rooms to surround them with interesting plants, install attractive paving or gravel underfoot, and supply comfortable furniture. As a final touch, a few attractive containers filled with sophisticated combinations of flowering plants will add both color and fragrance to the setting. ▪

1

Containers

Flowers in pots create flexible, temporary decorations that are ideal for livening up terraces and small sitting areas in which the expanse of paving or gravel underfoot is a bit colorless and monotonous to the eye. Decorate these outdoor rooms with large containers that complement the style of the house and the terrace, filled with annuals, perennials, or flowering bulbs. Use flower colors that harmonize with those of the facade, but choose the specific shades of those colors to create the atmosphere that you are looking for. Warm-colored flowers are great for animating a terrace facing north or in the shade of large trees. Cool shades, on the other hand, bring a sense of freshness to a spot bathed in sun. And garden containers have the great advantage of being flexible. You can change the decor from one year to the next, or even each season, by simply replacing the plants. ■

2

1. To give height to a container composition, use exotic specimens such as this cabbage palm (*Cordyline australis*), with ivy-leafed geraniums and licorice plant (*Helichrysum petiolare*) at its feet.

2. To brighten up a container, insert plants with variegated foliage like blue marguerite (*Felicia amelloides* 'Variegata'), whose leaves are bordered in cream.

3. In the terra-cotta urn, a spiky purple-leafed cabbage palm (*Cordyline australis*) rises through the white-edged green foliage of a graceful fuchsia. In the lower planter, the deep violet blossom of heliotrope (*Heliotropium peruvianum*) harmonizes with the mauve Swan River daisy (*Brachycome*), while white geraniums offer contrast.

3

Garden Retreats

Gardens often have little green corners where you can go to savor a few moments of calm. Sheltered from view and away from the main flow of traffic, these areas beg to be surrounded with flowering shrubs and perennials. Seen from afar, their touches of color will signal the presence of a secret retreat; up close, they will create an enchanted atmosphere with their delicate fragrance. Use shrubs or roses as a canvas of greenery against which a bed of perennials and annuals can glow. If you have a bench, let shrubs or climbers trained on a support provide an elegant backdrop behind it. Carpet the area with flowering groundcovers and low-growing herbs. For small sitting areas furnished with a table and chairs, in order to leave enough space to move easily around the furniture, limit yourself to planting only in beds around the perimeter of the area. Harmonize the colors of the plants with those of the environment, the materials used to pave the ground, and the furniture of the garden. Select plants that rebloom and are fragrant, but above all those that bloom from spring to autumn, when you are likely to linger here. Emphasize perennials, annuals, and bulbs, but also use shrubs and roses to make the place as attractive as possible. ■

Tips

All flowering plants attract wasps and bees, which are indispensable for pollinating them, and thus allowing the formation of fruit. But these insects are not always so welcome around a lounging area or a dining spot. Remember that certain species, called melliferous plants, especially attract them. These include shrubs like lavender, cotoneaster, caryopteris, butterfly bush, privet, burning bush, and tamarisk, as well as many perennials and annuals. Place such species away from sitting areas and terraces, where buzzing insects may make these areas inhospitable.

1. While flowering plants go a long way toward livening up a sitting space, do not forget to decorate these places with ornamental objects, accessories, and furniture to really give them panache. Antiques from a flea market give a supplementary touch of authenticity and charm.

Pages 84 & 85

1. Nestled in the shade of an ash tree, this bench invites the visitor to contemplate the rich arrangement of flowers and foliage that surrounds it.

2. Two rustic wooden benches face each other across a delicate perennial composition in shades of pink, white, and silver, comprising Miss Willmott's ghost (*Eryngium giganteum*), poppies, artemisia, roses, false dittany (*Ballota pseudodictamnus*), mallows, and hardy geraniums.

3 & 7. With smooth hydrangea (*Hydrangea arborescens* 'Annabelle') at its back, and climbing roses and a honeysuckle (*Lonicera x heckrotti*) on either side, this bench is nestled in the heart of an intimate garden spot surrounded by fragrant

plants. These aromatic herbs, among them lavender, catmint, thyme, and sage, remain decorative after flowering with their silver, yellow, or purple foliage.

4. Set in the center of the garden in an island of greenery, this little sitting area is both inundated with sun and sparkling with the colors of a climbing rose and numerous perennials.

5. The choice of one intense hue for furniture highlights its presence in the garden and produces a strong contrast with the surrounding vegetation—an original way to add a distinctive, creative design note to the whole.

6. This cobblestone-paved sitting area with stylish furniture is elegantly ornamented with climbing and shrub roses, but it is foliage color that sets it apart. The low, undulating hedge that surrounds the patio is sculpted of the luminous gilded foliage of golden box honeysuckle (*Lonicera nitida* 'Baggesen's Gold'). A dappled willow (*Salix integra* 'Hakuro Nishiki'), with its green leaves tinted with cream and pink, offers a striking contrast.

2

3

4

5

6

7

The Art of Camouflage

❋ **Use flowering plants to distract and conceal.** In the garden, a number of utilities or structures may need to be hidden from the eyes of visitors. Plants are the best way to effectively mask them, but a tall hedge or screen of shrubs can appear drab and monotonous, especially if the garden is small or the hedge is out of scale. Dress utilitarian spaces up a little with flowering plants, so that the eye sees a colorful composition instead of an ugly structure. ∎

Walls and Hedges

Like its vegetative counterpart, the hedge, a garden wall is often tall and imposing. Moreover, it can emphasize the limits of the garden in an arbitrary and overbearing way. To soften a wall's effect, you might just create a border against it; if the wall itself is attractive, it can even serve as a nice backdrop. On the other hand, if the wall is less than elegant, cover it with climbing plants or place roses or large shrubs in front of it, and then plant perennials and annuals in front of them to create a sloping bank of greenery. Don't forget to insert a few evergreens to animate the scene during winter. When an existing hedge separates two gardens, it already forms a useful backdrop that needs only embellishing with flowering plants. A border of shrubs, roses, and perennials can be created in front of it, in descending order of height. In both cases, think of leaving a path two feet or so wide between the border and the hedge or wall, to allow you to work from behind the border. ∎

1. A perennial border placed below a climbing rose helps it to soften an old wall. Under a large specimen of butterfly rose (*Rosa mutabilis*), a carpet of garden pinks (*Dianthus*) creates a base from which emerge the taller stems of balloon flower (*Platycodon grandiflorus* 'Album') and white foxglove (*Digitalis purpurea* 'Alba').

2. Drawing the eye away from a brick wall and a hedge of oleaster (*Elaeagnus x ebbingei*), this large bed sparkles with an ensemble of yellow-flowered perennials, composed of lady's mantle (*Alchemilla mollis*), daylilies, and yarrow (*Achillea* 'Coronation Gold'), with the blue-mauve of balloon flower (*Platycodon grandiflorus*) striking a contrasting note.

3 & 4. Mixed borders hide a wall and a hedge with a tall bank of plants made up of a first tier of low-growing perennials and a higher tier of bushy perennials and shrubs.

2

3

4

2

3

4

Steep Slopes

When a garden is built on sloping ground, it is not always easy to handle the differences in the levels without resorting to covering steep banks with a single type of plant, chosen from among a limited range of groundcovers. Yet sloping ground can be a real asset, making it possible to create dramatic compositions in which all the plants are visible at once. When they grow on the natural slope of hilly terrain, plants produce a cascading effect, revealing a much more interesting quality than if they were crowded together in a flat border. If the slope is very steep, you will need to use rocks or a low wall to anchor the earth and keep it from eroding away. Creating a terraced staircase effect also simplifies planting and upkeep. Terrace walls or rocks steps will be hidden underneath the foliage and flowers, while still maintaining their indispensable role of stabilizing the soil. If you are dealing with a gentle slope, on the other hand, it will not be necessary to go to such lengths; just remember to create a little level platform around each plant so that water does not run off. To plant on a bank, give priority to low perennials that have a ground-covering habit, such as traditional rock garden plants. These will create a spreading mat of leaves and flowers that will rapidly cover the slope. To give more

height and relief to the composition, combine these with small shrubs or dwarf conifers like junipers and firs. Save a few spaces to tuck in spring-flowering bulbs, annuals, or aromatic herbs that will complement your color scheme. Finally, by playing with the heights of the plants themselves, you can modify the contours of the slope, at least visually. Where the slope is very steep, use flowering plants that are tall and solid at the bottom of the bank, and set flat or shorter plants at the top: In this way, it is possible to create an illusion that the slope is gentler than it really is. ∎

1. The cascading waves of flowers and foliage of the perennials planted on this bank soften and conceal its terraced slope.

2. In this rock garden, annuals like the glowing orange African daisy (*Arctotis* 'Harlequin') coexist happily with perennials such as daylilies and rose campion (*Lychnis coronaria*), with its deep rose flowers and silvery stems. And then there are shrubs—*Spiraea japonica* 'Little Princess,' with its soft pink flowers, and the golden-leaved *S. japonica* 'Goldmound,' set off by the deep bronze foliage of purple ninebark (*Physocarpus opulifolius* 'Diabolo').

3. Euphorbias, hardy geraniums, artemisias, catmints, and alchemillas cover a bank that slopes down to a stream, creating an elegant patchwork of cool and acidic shades.

4. Cascades of Cape marigolds (*Dimorphotheca*), blue marguerites (*Felicia amelloides*), and African daisies (*Arctotis*) hide the surface of a retaining wall, while also making the viewer forget the difference in level.

Screens and Dividers

In a garden, it is not always easy to define distinct areas without creating a boxed-in feeling, or to enclose a space without cutting off the view of the surrounding scenery. However, substantial mixed beds of shrubs and perennials offer a colorful alternative to traditional tall, monotonous hedges. If necessary, begin by consulting with your neighbors about planting larger shrubs or trees, and about any decorative structures, such as arches or trellises, that you wish to install on the border to make a more effective screen. Then design a border that will look attractive on both sides, perhaps one inspired by English mixed borders, if you use chiefly perennials, or flowering hedges, if you prefer ornamental shrubs. When the garden borders on a public space, why not allow for glimpses of the other side? And if the garden needs to be enclosed to restrict access, why not hide wrought-iron or wooden fencing inside the border? ∎

1. Dusty miller, broom, and California lilac (*Ceanothus*), among other perennials and shrubs, make up the substance of this screening border, which divides the edge of the garden from the surrounding landscape in a very informal, natural style.

2. Against a hydrangea hedge topping a fence that marks the neighbor's property, a screening border of roses flanked with perennials, such as *Gaura lindheimeri*, annual poppies, snow-in-summer (*Cerastium tomentosum*), marguerite daisies (*Chrysanthemum frutescens*), and false dittany (*Ballota pseudo-dictamnus*), lends a charming bucolic air to the garden's perimeter.

3. Backed against a bowered hedge and punctuated by columns of yew, this mixed border cleverly masks the boundaries of the garden with a pageantry rich in hue and sophistication.

4. Trained over an enclosing fence, the pliant stalks of climbing roses weave an organic curtain that hides the edge of the garden with a torrent of flowers, underlined in turn by the deep rose shades of garden pinks.

5. Rising from a bed of hydrangeas and annuals, this trellislike metal structure, installed to define the edges of the property, welcomes climbing roses and elegantly indicates the border between two gardens.

2

3

4

5

Embellishing the Garden

※ **Planting flowers to make a garden simply more beautiful.** Using flowering plants, whether perennials, annuals, bulbs, or even shrubs, is the easiest way to add color to a garden and is much more pleasant than enclosing it with a wall or a painted fence. They can adorn paths, enliven garden ornaments, or brighten up a glade and are easy to plant and to work with. Begin by introducing a few small notes of harmonious color, then let these shades spread through a border. Suddenly, the garden has a completely new look! ■

Walkways and Allées

The main walkways of a property are used so frequently, it makes sense to liven up the area around them. Begin by planting islands of shrubs and perennials near the beginning and end of a route. If it is a winding path, tuck flowers into its curves to create length and mystery. Start with a few notes of color, and take the time to see the effect of these before you launch into full-blown flower borders. Remember also that the longer the path, the more work it will take to maintain beds along it and keep it looking nice. Choose perennials over annuals, as perennials can live for many years, often propagate rapidly, and smother weeds. In addition, selecting plants adapted to your soil and region will give you a better chance of having a garden filled with healthy plants. Finally, adopt natural gardening techniques, such as mulching your beds and using beneficial plant associations to combat parasites.

2

1. This cobblestone-paved walk makes its way through a carpet of perennials such as Siberian spurge (*Euphorbia seguieriana* ssp. *niciciana*) staggered along alternating sides of the path.

2. Space out the bloom times to make sure a path is colorful throughout the year. Here, after the phlox has finished blooming, the more subtle grasses will take over.

3. Let plants billow out into an otherwise neatly defined path sometimes, as here, where the lax stems of valerian soften a walkway's austerity.

3

Footpaths

Much narrower than the grander walkways, footpaths make up the secondary network of traffic in the garden. They are great for creating shortcuts or allowing the gardener access for tending to otherwise hard-to-reach plantings. Grassy paths should be well maintained. Otherwise, completely remove the grass and, to make the bare paths more comfortable to walk on, cover them with a layer of wood chips, fine sand, or gravel. Always opt for materials that are simple, have a natural appearance, and differentiate small footpaths from the principal walkways. Avoid paving stones, bricks, or cobblestones, which have too much of an official feeling and make it hard to modify the path if needed. These paths may turn out to be temporary, soon to be taken over by plants. To cultivate the mystery that surrounds small, meandering footpaths, allow plants to spill over the path, obscuring it almost completely every now and then. You can also cover the paths themselves with carpets of ground-hugging herbs, like thyme or chamomile, that will release their fragrance with every step. If you obscure footpaths behind screens of foliage and flowers, however, always keep the end of the path in view. In other words, create a landmark to head for at path's end, such as a garden ornament or an inviting bench, which will be especially helpful for visitors who do not know the garden and its secret recesses. ■

Tips

Use ground-covering plants to hide the edges of a footpath. The species traditionally known as rock plants are perfect for this. Some, like wild thyme, saxifrages, sedums, pussytoes (*Antennaria dioica*), or mountain sandwort (*Arenaria montana*), will form a dense, low-growing carpet. Plant a second tier a little farther back with larger species, such as basket-of-gold (*Alyssum saxatile*), candytuft (*Iberis sempervirens*), wall bell-flower (*Campanula portenschladiana*), sun roses (*Helianthemum*), purple rock cress (*Aubrieta*), snow-in-summer (*Cerastium tomentosum*), maiden pink (*Dianthus deltoids*), and moss pink (*Phlox subulata*). Finally, more substantial perennials like lady's mantle (*Alchemilla*), artemisia, heath asters, or hardy geraniums can be placed farther back, around the base of shrubs and very large perennials.

1 & 5. When softening the line of a footpath, do not hide it completely. There must be a visual contact with its end. In these gardens, the house and the bench at the end of the paths remain quite visible although the path is overgrown.

2. Ornamental allium, catmint (*Nepeta* x *faassenii*), and lavender cotton (*Santolina rosmarinifolia* 'Primrose Gem') line a network of footpaths whose inter-sections are signaled by obelisks of woven bands of steel that have been patinated by time.

3. Planted at the foot of peonies and roses, the milky blue flowers of catmint sprawl over this grassy footpath. When they have finished blooming, they will be cut back hard to encourage them to remain compact and decorative up to autumn.

4. Clumps of lavender have been allowed to spill over into this foot-path; the curves thus formed disguise its original line and give it a more sinuous and natural feel that is very attractive.

6. The poppies, wall-flowers, forget-me-nots, and pansies that line this path only bloom in the spring. These biennials will be replaced in May with annuals that flower from July to October.

1

2

3

4

5

6

Garden Stairs

1. In the mountains, a garden path and stone stairway are inspired by natural fallen rocks. Here, carefully set rocks serve as steps, but their irregular contour leaves large fissures from which sprout alpine plants like sedum, saxifrages, or hardy geranium (*Geranium* x *cantabrigiense*), in the foreground here, whose seed heads have great ornamental value even after the plants have finished blooming.

2. To soften the effect of the stone, one side of these stairs is covered with ground-hugging perennials like yellow pheasant's eye (*Adonis vernalis*) and the pink shades of sea thrift (*Armeria maritime*), evening primrose (*Oenothera speciosa*), and stone cress (*Aethionema armenum* 'Warley Rose'). On the other side, golden conifers and yellow flowering shrubs, such as St.-John's-wort (*Hypericum patulum* 'Hidcote'), echo this wave of colors.

In a sloped garden, stairs connect the different levels and allow access from one to another. Their lines should be simple and functional, and the number of steps kept to a strict minimum. Even then, these structures can create an obstacle—a danger, even—for children, the aged, and the handicapped, and make it harder to maneuver wheelbarrows, lawnmowers, and the like around the garden. Therefore, whenever possible, it is best to create an alternative path with a gentle slope. Stone steps in the garden will produce a dramatic, monumental effect that can overwhelm plantings, so allow plenty of space around them for shrubs, conifers, perennials, and climbing plants to soften their angles and edges and better blend them with their surroundings. Finally, consider lighting stairways with lampposts or spotlights set in the ground to make them safer at night. Place a light every five or six steps on each side to illuminate the stairway evenly. Stairways that are rarely used are often, over time, transformed into decorative ornaments in their own right. The individual steps, no longer under the constraints of function and safety, will become so many platforms on which it is tempting to place pots and tubs holding flowering plants that, because they are above ground level, will be prominently visible. Use annuals, bulbs, and aromatic herbs in these containers; their short life span allows you to change the look at will. In some cases, when stone steps are made of porous rock and worn by time, the fissures and fractures that form make ideal homes for wind-borne self-seeders. Various mosses, maidenhair fern (*Adiantum* ■ ■ ■

Tips

To create an easy-to-use stairway, there are a few principles you must follow. First and foremost, apply the following rule: Twice the height of the riser plus the depth of one tread should together equal twenty-four inches. A landing every seven to eight steps will let people catch their breath before continuing. Finally, when the grade is gentle, it is best to create a succession of wide landings rather than a set of stairs. Not only does this make the going much easier, but the effect is much more elegant.

1

2

■ ■ ■

pedatum), maidenhair spleenwort (*Asplenium trichomanes*), and fleabane (*Erigeron karvinskianus*) can drive their roots into cracks in the stone steps and weave a veil of foliage and flowers over them. These plants present no threat to the integrity of the stone. In contrast, shrubs and creeping perennials with woody roots can weaken stairs by dislodging the treads and therefore must be regularly watched for and pulled out. Dressing stairs with greenery can fundamentally change their look. Some pots placed here and there will transform the rigid rectilinear lines of a staircase into a sinuous path that is attractive to the eye. ■

1. The austerity of this classically built stairway, flanked by two carved stone corbels topped with baskets of fruit, is softened by the exuberance of a small-flowered rose and the lavender-blue flowers of catmint (*Nepeta* x *faassenii*), in turn set off by a silvery Scotch thistle (*Onopordon acanthium*) and the emerald green leaves of hellebores.

2. A border of culinary sage (*Salvia officinalis*), planted in the ground at the base of roses and figs, makes a transition between the stairs and the ground. In front of the stairs, a succession of pots accommodate a luminous shower tree (*Cassia corymbosa*), tufts of everlasting (*Helichrysum italicum* ssp. *serotinum*), with its pretty silver foliage, heliotrope (*Heliotropium peruvianum*), and bee balm (*Monarda* 'Cambridge Scarlet').

3. Fleabane (*Erigeron karvinskianus*), with flowers that resemble miniature daisies, sows itself everywhere, not limiting itself to the soil: On the stair steps themselves, it sprouts out of fissures between the stone slabs.

1

2

Arbors and Pergolas

Wooden or iron frames, built to decorate an allée or to provide shade for a small sitting area, can also serve as supports for climbing plants—not only hardy climbers like honeysuckle, clematis, wisteria, or Virginia creeper, but also more tender twining plants such as jasmine, passionflower, solanums, and bougainvillea. That's not to mention annuals, such as morning glories and sweet peas, which are quite valuable for their quick growth and generous flowering. Plant one at the base of each arbor pilaster and train the stems with wire as they grow. With most perennial climbers, you may have to wait a year or two for the first flowers. Finally, to amplify the decorative effect and to extend the flowering season, combine several species and allow them to weave together. ■

Tips

Pergolas are generally built with treated lumber to protect them from weather and wood-eating insects. But be careful about any anchoring points in the ground: They support the entire structure, whose weight (branches, foliage, flowers) will increase through the years. If they are in permanent contact with moist soil, they risk being damaged. To prevent this from happening, manufacturers suggest fitting the vertical pieces into metal ends that are planted in the ground or sealed in a base of concrete.

1. A wooden pergola has many uses; here, it marks the end point of the perspective that is created along a grassy walkway and provides shade for a small sitting area. Partially covered with climbing roses, it offers a glimpse into another part of the garden, highlighting the plants beyond as a frame highlights a picture.

2. In this garden, a pergola covers a large gravel walkway and supports a collection of climbing roses and clematis. The posts are linked together by a bower hedge that separates the zones of circulation from the beds made of old roses and decorated with blue oat grass (*Helictotrichon sempervirens*) and goatsbeard (*Aruncus dioicus* 'Glasnevin').

3. Arches are used to give shelter to a walkway and support climbing plants. Here, wire mesh arches make it easier to train the roses.

The Large Garden

When a garden covers a large area, and you would like more flowering plants and less lawn, it is most effective to plant large swaths of the same species: In addition to creating a bold visual effect, such plantings demand less maintenance than mixed borders made of a number of varieties. Let yourself find inspiration in the principles of planting in waves or rows. Create generous islands, each filled with only one variety of plant, chosen to suit the style of your garden. These should be planted only after you have properly prepared the soil. To prevent weeds from sprouting at the same time as your new plantings and to keep the soil moist, put down landscape cloth before planting. While you wait for the plants to grow and cover the entire bed, keep it well covered with mulch. The success of this style of planting chiefly depends on the choice of appropriate plants. Select vigorous perennials or shrubs that will grow rapidly, being especially careful to choose those best suited to the soil and

climate of your region. Among the perennials, concentrate on species that spread by underground runners, like loosestrife (*Lythrum virgatum*), garden loosestrife (*Lysimachia punctata*), ornamental or culinary sage (*Salvia*), tickseed (*Coreopsis*), speedwell (*Veronica*), asters, or coneflower (*Rudbeckia*); many ornamental grasses also fall into this category. Other plants that are well known for spreading quickly are ground covers. This is the case with lamb's ears (*Stachys*), lady's mantle (*Alchemilla*), hardy geraniums, St.-John's-wort (*Hypericum patulum*), and catmint (*Nepeta*). All of these plants are easy to increase by dividing them in spring or autumn. This is a great to fill out your garden inexpensively. As for maintenance, just cut back the dried stems at the end of winter. ■

2

1 & 2. To fill large spaces with flowers, create massive groupings of single varieties. Here, lavender-blue catmint (*Nepeta x faassenii* 'Six Hills Giant'), the silver-leafed spikes of lamb's ear (*Stachys lanata* 'Silver Carpet'), pink hardy geraniums (*Geranium endressii* 'Wargrave Pink'), cottage pink (*Dianthus plumarius* 'Annabel'), and the pale spikes of *Sisyrinchium striatum* create a grand tapestry of colors that suits the scale of this large garden.

3. When planting in the wave style, make sure to carefully orchestrate bloom times. Here, masterwort (*Astrantia major*) and ornamental salvias are in full bloom, but the asters and phlox still show only foliage. To soften the whole and bridge the perennial groupings, add swaths of ornamental grasses.

Shade Plantings

The shady areas of a garden are often difficult to fill with flowers. There are perennials that are well suited to these situations, but you will have more options if you begin by high-pruning trees to remove low branches above your beds, then thin out the higher branches to allow some shafts of light to come through from above. By increasing the amount of light, you widen your choice of plants to include those that enjoy partial shade. Give priority to species whose natural habitat is the woodland understory. For perennials, the choice is vast: monkshood, bugle, Japanese anemones, goatsbeard (*Aruncus dioicus*), astilbes, forget-me-nots, euphorbias, meadowsweet (*Filipendula ulmaria*), primrose, daylilies, and hardy geraniums. Some shrubs, like serviceberry, azaleas, rhododendrons, dogwoods, hydrangeas, star magnolias, elders, lilacs, and viburnums, are equally adapted to semi-shaded areas. Finally, most spring-flowering bulbs do well in clearings and under shrubs and trees; since they grow and flower when other plants haven't yet leafed out, the understory will be at its most sun-filled. When the shrubs have leafed out, the bulbs have already finished their growth and their leaves have begun to die back. ■

1. In an orchard where the trees are well enough spaced out, numerous perennials can flourish; white ox-eye daisies (*Leucanthemum vulgare* 'May Queen'), pastel rose masterwort (*Astrantia major* 'Rosea'), orange daylily (*Hemerocallis* 'Burning Daylight'), and yellow yarrow (*Achillea* 'Coronation Gold').

2. Narcissus and biennials like forget-me-nots benefit from the sun that filters through trees and flourish among the lilac-pink honesty (*Lunaria rediviva*) and white dame's rocket (*Hesperis matronalis* 'Alba Plena').

Index

Index of Plant Names